THE CIVIL WAR

Literature Units, Projects, and Activities

Written by Janet Cassidy
Edited by Sheila Wolinsky

SCHOLASTIC
PROFESSIONAL BOOKS

NEW YORK • TORONTO • LONDON • AUCKLAND • SYDNEY

*For Patrick Francis Cassidy and his brother Charles,
who fought on opposite sides in the Civil War.*

"The Bloodiest War" from THE CIVIL WAR by Timothy Levi Biel.
Copyright © 1991 by Lucent Books, Inc. Reprinted by permission.

Pages 56-62 were adapted from the screenplay for *Glory*, by Kevin Jarre, copyright © 1989, a Tri-Star Pictures Release of a Freddie Fields Production of an Edward Zwick Film. Used by permission of Kevin Jarre.

Interior design by Jacqueline Swensen
Cover and interior illustrations by Mona Mark
Cover design by Vincent Ceci

ISBN 0-590-49509-7

12 11 10 9 8 7 6 5 4   6/9

Printed in the U.S.A.

TABLE OF CONTENTS

Library of Congress

Introduction 4

SECTION ONE:

Making It Work. 5

THE UNION VOLUNTEER.

SECTION TWO:
The Literature

The Bloodiest War (An essay) . . 16

Across Five Aprils 19

Lincoln: A Photobiography 31

The Boys' War 39

Behind Rebel Lines 45

Undying Glory 51

Bull Run 63

SECTION THREE:

Putting It All Together 69

Additional Resources. 78

Library of Congress

INTRODUCTION

I remember very little about the history I studied as an elementary school student, except a vague blur of names and dates. I must have "learned" it, because my report cards showed good grades, but since what I learned was unconnected with anything in my life, it was soon forgotten.

It wasn't until years later, when I began researching my family tree, that I became really interested in history. During the 1850s, my great-great-grandfather was raising his family in Washington, D.C. Photos of Washington taken during this time show unfinished buildings and muddy streets. I pictured my ancestor walking there.

I read that Lincoln had attended a funeral at a church in Georgetown and the sexton, who had been instructed not to admit anyone until the President had arrived, failed to recognize Lincoln and at first would not let him in. With a thrill, I realized that the sexton was my ancestor. When the war broke out, two of this man's sons signed up to fight—on opposite sides of the conflict. From military service records, I learned the Union brother had fought in the Battle of Wilson's Creek—and a tiny spot in Missouri I had never heard of before became important to me. After the war, the other brother moved north to find work. According to a family story, he hung the Confederate flag out his window every 4th of July. I wondered how his New Jersey neighbors reacted— the war was as fresh in people's minds then as Vietnam is to us today.

So history became, instead of meaningless names and dates and places, stories—the stories of my family.

Children love stories. What better way then, to hook them on history than through historical fiction? Through the pages of historical fiction, the past comes alive. The past is the story of people who are no less real because they are fictional. Through these fictional characters, children relive the past vicariously, and gain knowledge about the values, hardships, and beliefs of a period. They learn about events that have affected the present.

Children love stories. But as they struggle to make sense of the world, they also ask, "Is this real? Did this really happen?" Well-written biographies, such as Russell Friedman's *Lincoln: A Photobiography*, offer children the chance to get to know the people whose stories changed America. Through quality nonfiction, such as Jim Murphy's *The Boys' War*, children read the stories of ordinary people reacting to the extraordinary events we now call history.

We hope this sample unit will make the task of using literature to teach the story of the Civil War easier, and a rewarding experience for you and your students.

—*Janet Cassidy*

SECTION ONE:

MAKING IT WORK

Ask teachers why they use trade books to teach history, and you'll probably get similar answers: Well-chosen books provide students with a vicarious understanding of the past; they spark imaginations and present exciting paths to explore; they provide numerous opportunities for building students' critical reading and thinking skills.

Why, then, don't more teachers use high quality works of fiction and nonfiction to heighten students' interest in history and enhance their learning experience? Many of your colleagues would probably offer the same response: A literature-based history unit does not just happen; it requires a great deal of preparation time.

If the above concern has dampened your enthusiasm for using trade books to teach or supplement instruction on the Civil War, this Resource Book is for you. To learn the specifics, take some time to flip through this book. As you do so, keep the following in mind:

- The suggested literature and teaching strategies represent a sample unit on the Civil War.

- Instruction can be organized in a variety of ways.

- Our unit is based on a cooperative approach in which groups of five or six students each read and discuss a different core book over a period of one to two weeks.

- During sessions, students complete a prepared set of study guide questions and specific literature-related activities.

If you do not feel comfortable with this approach, please remember that most of our suggestions can be altered to fit your teaching style. Many other books, questions, and sets of activities are also possible and, ultimately, you may decide to substitute other core books, change the questions, or add ideas of your own. In this section, we offer some practical advice that can help you make those substitutions, additions, and changes. The following suggestions can also help to answer the most important question of all: How can you construct a Civil War theme unit that works for both you *and* your students?

GETTING STARTED

A first step in preparing any theme-based unit is to decide how much time you want to spend on the unit. Second, you will need to decide your instructional objectives. Next, you'll want to gather literature that supports your teaching goals.

Begin by taking a closer look at the works described in Section Two. Summaries have been provided for six core books—two works of historical fiction, two informational books, and two biographies. Numerous other titles are described throughout the text. As you read about each book, ask yourself questions like these: Can it help me fulfill my instructional goals? Is it of interest to my students? Will it generate discussion?

Try to pick five or six books that meet these criteria. In addition, you may also want to think about the following considerations:

- Do the core books represent a wide variety of authors, genres, and writing styles?
- Do these books span a broad range of reading levels to ensure that all students can find a book to match their abilities?

※ CIVIL WAR RESOURCE CENTER

Once the core books have been selected, collect five or six copies of each title. Place your classroom library on an easily accessible shelf. Additional works of fiction that are "too good to miss" can be arranged on a table in a quiet corner of the classroom and used for outside or leisure reading. To make this reading center more inviting, you might add a comfortable couch, chairs, or pillows.

A resource center puts reference materials on the topic at your students' fingertips, and allows them to readily explore the people, places, and events they are reading about. Stock this center with some of the high quality nonfiction books highlighted throughout the unit. As students explore and do research on their own, encourage them to add reference materials that they find to be especially interesting or helpful. Other possibilities include:

- *A Nation Torn: The Story of How the Civil War Began* by Delia Ray (Lodestar, 1990) Grades 5–8. Letters, diaries, eyewitness accounts, and vintage photos are used to chronicle the crucial events that led to the war and nearly destroyed the Republic.

- *The Civil War* by Timothy Levi Biel (Lucent Books, 1991) Grades 5–8. A compelling essay on the war and its devastating effects introduces this

6

examination of the political, cultural, and military aspects of the conflict. Chapters include: "The Roots of War," "An Unavoidable Conflict," "Amateurs at War," "The Western Road to Shiloh," "Robert E. Lee: A New Confederate Hero," "Closing the Vise," and "The Death of the Confederacy."

◆ *Civil War!: America Becomes One Nation* by James I. Robertson, Jr. (Knopf, 1992) Grades 5–8. This concise, well-balanced overview focuses on the general political issues that preceded the war and then provides a chronological account of the major events of the conflict.

◆ *The Civil War* by Eric Weiner (Smithmark, 1992) Grades 4–6. Packed with information and illustrations, this overview is written in a lively style that will attract and delight browsers.

◆ *First Battles*, edited by Carter Smith (Millbrook, 1993) Grades 5–8. This pictorial history begins with the first battle at Fort Sumter in April 1861 and ends with the Battle of Fredericksburg, which took place late in 1862. Numerous illustrations and short chapters make this volume a good choice for reluctant readers with an interest in the Civil War.

◆ *The Civil War: An Illustrated History*, edited by Geoffrey C. Ward, Ric Burns & Ken Burns (Knopf, 1990) Grade 7 and up. This companion volume to the celebrated PBS television documentary *The Civil War* offers 475 images that bring the world of the 1860s to life. The text is often accompanied by the voices of the people who lived during these war-torn years. Five essays by leading historians add another dimension to this glowing work.

In this center for exploration, you might also include photos, maps, audio and video equipment, a computer and printer, and bulletin boards for displaying your students' work. Another bulletin board might be used to display quotations and passages that students found to be especially moving or effective. To start this display going, post some of your favorite "Quotables." Below are some examples. You will probably find many others as you read the materials you will assign for this unit.

"Slavery is an unqualified evil to the Negro, to the white man, to the soil, and to the state."
—Abraham Lincoln

"It is well that war is so terrible or we should grow too fond of it."
—General Robert E. Lee

"This war was a fearful lesson and should teach us the necessity of avoiding war in the future."
—General Ulysses S. Grant

"The air seemed filled with the iron missiles, and the forest trees were riven…The birds seemed confused, and would fly down and light on the heads and knapsacks of the soldiers; rabbits would come out from under the bushes and hide under the soldiers' coats."
—Sergeant Henry C. Morhous,
123rd Regiment, NY,
on the third and final day of Pickett's
Charge at the Battle of Gettysburg

"After each fight, I would search the field for anyone…who did not require the use of his equipment. I must confess to feeling very bad doing this, believing the dead should not be disturbed, but I had no other course."

—A 16-year-old soldier in
Jim Murhpy's *The Boys' War*

⊞ ACTIVATING PRIOR KNOWLEDGE

If students are already familiar with this historical period, the Civil War Quotables display can be used as a quick and easy way to introduce the unit and activate prior knowledge. Begin by explaining how and why you selected these quotes and passages.

Then pick three or four and tell why each one is special to you. Encourage students to share their own responses. Next, focus on each quote at a time, asking questions that provide a chance for students to share what they know of the war and its causes. For example, if you display the quotes on this and the preceding page, you might ask:

- ◆ Why did many Northerners believe that slavery was an "unqualified evil"? Did all Northerners agree with Lincoln's statement? What were some of the arguments offered by people who were for slavery? Was slavery the only issue that caused the two halves of the country to clash?

- ◆ Who were Robert E. Lee and Ulysses S. Grant? What other famous names do you associate with the Civil War?

- ◆ Have you ever heard of Pickett's Charge? Why is the Battle of Gettysburg famous? What other battles do you know about?

- ◆ Based on the two soldiers' quotes, what adjectives would you use to describe the Civil War? What do you think it was like to be a soldier on the front lines?

After the discussion, divide the class into cooperative learning groups. Ask each group to make a list of all the things they already know about the Civil War. Students can then work together to list people, places, battles, events, and issues they want to investigate. This second list can be used as a guide for independent exploration in the resource center.

⊞ DEVELOPING NEEDED BACKGROUND

If prior knowledge is weak, use the first day of the unit to provide needed background knowledge. To aid you in this task, we have reprinted the "The Bloodiest War" on pages 16–18. This compelling introduction from Timothy Levi Biel's *The Civil War* can be read aloud to the class.

After listening, provide time for a whole group activity. Begin by asking students to tell about some of the important things they just learned. As each volunteer responds, write his or her fact on a section of the chalkboard, under the heading **What We Know**. Next, ask individuals to share questions that occurred to them as they listened to "The Bloodiest War." Write these questions on a second section of the chalkboard, under the heading **What We Want to Find Out**. If students have a difficult time getting started, reread the introduction, or offer some examples from the chart that follows.

WHAT WE KNOW	WHAT WE WANT TO FIND OUT
The Civil War claimed 620,000 lives— more than all other U.S. wars combined.	*Why did so many people die? How were they killed? Are there other statistics? Are they equally frightening?*
More than half the soldiers not killed were wounded or taken prisoner.	*What kind of treatment did the wounded receive? What were prison camps like?*
Shiloh, Antietam, and Gettysburg were especially bloody battles.	*Why were these battles so bloody? What are some other famous battles?*
General Lee led the Southern army; General Grant led the Northern army.	*Were they good leaders? What were some of their victories and defeats?*
Many families were torn apart by the war.	*Why were they torn apart? How were ordinary people affected?*
The Civil War did not start out as a war to end slavery.	*What started the war?*
The Emancipation Proclamation was issued on January 1, 1863.	*What did it say? How did slaves react? How did pro-slavery people feel?*
Memorials of the war and its soldiers are all over America.	*Where are they? What do they look like?*
More than 100 million Americans have ancestors who were affected by the war.	*Do I have a Civil War ancestor?*

PLEASE NOTE: Statements and questions about the Reconstruction period have been omitted because the primary goal of this sample unit is to provide students with a thorough understanding of the war years (1861–1865) and the tragic and devastating nature of the conflict. In many cases, the suggested literature can also be used to introduce or review the issues and events that sparked the war.

As students read the materials for this unit, they will discover the answers to many of their questions. Provide a space where they can share this information. This may be a third section of the chalkboard labeled **What We Learned**. Another option is to cover a large section of a wall with sheets of shelf paper or oaktag. This ongoing display can also be used as a place for students to record and share any interesting or startling facts or statistics they find as they read. To get this display going, you or a student volunteer might enter some of the frightening statistics included in "The Bloodiest War."

▨ AN ONGOING TIME LINE

This ongoing K-W-L activity serves several functions: It leads students to read purposefully and actively; helps tie all the individual reading together; and motivates students to get involved—and stay involved—throughout the unit. An ongoing time line can be used to achieve the same goals.

Before assigning the whole group activity, decide on the time period you want your students to cover. For example, they might begin with the first battle at Ft. Sumter on April 12, 1861 and end with Lee's surrender to Grant at Appomattox on April 9, 1965. Another option is to start this chronology with Abraham Lincoln's election in November of 1860, include information about the Confederate states that seceded as a result of the election, and end with Lincoln's assassination on April 14, 1865.

To provide students with a greater understanding of how the issues of slavery and states' rights combined to spark the war, suggest that they begin with 1819, the year the people of the Missouri Territory sought statehood and voted to permit slavery. At that time, slavery was illegal in half of the country's twenty-two states and legal in the other half. Because Northern Congressmen did not want to upset the balance between free and slave states, the House of Representatives passed a bill declaring that Missouri could only enter the Union if it banned slavery. This was called the Missouri Compromise. Students can use the reference materials in the resource center to learn more about this controversy. As they research, they should also look for information about the Compromise of 1850, the Kansas-Nebraska Act (1854), and the Dred Scott decision (1857).

At the end of the unit, students can use the L (what we learned) section of the K-W-L chart and their time line to help them complete many of the projects described in the PUTTING IT ALL TOGETHER section of this Resource Book. Throughout Section Two, you'll also find numerous follow-up activities that can give students a head start with end-of-unit projects. These project connections appear in boldface type.

▨ OPTIONS AND STRATEGIES FOR MANAGING THE UNIT

Teacher-directed projects and activities have been provided to help you motivate interest in reading and research, integrate various content areas, and engage students in critical thinking about the materials they have read. To ensure that all students can respond to the literature in a mode they feel comfortable with, a variety of individual and small group activities have been suggested.

Student-directed projects might also be offered as an option to students. Students who have been in traditional classrooms may be unaccustomed to this much freedom, and may need help in getting started, brainstorming, selecting an idea, and gathering information. Allowing students to contribute to the planning of the unit may involve taking some risks and, at the onset, it may require some additional work on your part. However, many teachers have found that this approach also has numerous benefits: It allows students to go well beyond the expectations of the person or people who designed the unit; promotes a feeling of ownership and interest in the entire classroom; and lets students know that your room is a place for exploration, trial and error, and imagination.

Dialog journals are another popular option. Students respond in writing to the ideas and events in their core book, and the teacher or a peer group member makes a written response. If you choose this option, have each student bring in a spiral-bound notebook, or make dialog journals by stapling together sheets of paper. Encourage students to write in their journals every day.

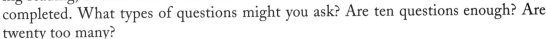

ASKING QUESTIONS

There's no question about it. You can enhance the reading experience even more by sharing some questions during reading, or after a book has been completed. What types of questions might you ask? Are ten questions enough? Are twenty too many?

Those are all good questions. The answers will vary from book to book, depending on:

◆ the length and/or difficulty level of the book;

◆ the ability level of your students;

◆ your teaching philosophy and style.

Because all of these variables must be taken into account, we have provided two very different sets of questions for four of the six core books in this unit. **Chapter-by-chapter guided reading questions** have been included for students who may require teacher support while reading *Across Five Aprils, Lincoln: A Photobiography, The Boys' War,* and *Undying Glory.* The lesson plans for these titles also include **independent reading questions** that can be used with students who can read these books on their own. *Behind Rebel Lines* is a simply written, adventure-packed biography. Most of your students will have little or no trouble getting through it, so only independent reading questions have been suggested to help students share and discuss what they have learned after reading this book. *Bull Run* is another special case. A special lesson plan has been provided for this unusual and innovative historical novel.

In all cases, the discussion questions provided are meant as a guide only. Use them as "jumping-off points," and encourage students to write or ask their own questions. Be open to where students' ideas take the discussion.

BOOKTALKS AND STUDENT SELECTION

Students will be more motivated to respond to these questions if they are allowed to select the book they will study. To facilitate student choice, give a booktalk in which you enthusiastically describe each of the core books in the unit. You might begin by giving a brief synopsis of the book, then build student interest by posing a question that calls for a personal response, or one that helps students relate the content of the book to their own experiences. The **Summary** and **Creating Interest** sections that begin each lesson plan can be used to help you prepare your script. To add variety to your talk, you might also share a passage from one of the books or describe an incident or scene that you found to be particularly exciting or moving.

At the culmination of the booktalk, ask individuals to select the book they want to read. If too many students want the same title, a lottery system can be used to decide who gets the book. Point out that if students don't get their first choice, they can read the book as outside reading. Also mention that many wonderful historical novels are available in the reading center. These works of fiction can also be used for outside or leisure reading.

WORKING WITH LITERATURE GROUPS

Next, ask students to form groups based on the books they have chosen. After the books have been distributed, suggest that students preview their book by reading the chapter headings and browsing through the photographs. Invite them to formulate two or three questions they hope the book will answer.

Purposes can also be set by asking students to complete a study guide containing the questions you have chosen for the book. Suggest that group members go over their study guides together. Make sure they understand that answering the questions is a requirement for the unit. Then provide a large block of class time for silent reading, or suggest that students bring their books home and start them that night.

After two or three days of independent reading, meet with each group for a 20- to 30-minute discussion. During this first meeting, encourage students to share their initial reactions to the book. As they talk, listen for signs of any individual group member who is experiencing difficulty. Based on the outcome of this discussion, you may wish to assign an activity to enhance or extend students' understanding of the book.

Group members should meet every day to share what they have enjoyed and learned from their book. These meetings can also be used as a time for students to share what they have written in their dialog journals and discuss responses to the study guide questions. Questions can be answered in writing or orally. If the latter option is chosen, you may wish to assign a group leader within each group to take notes. The group leader can be changed every day.

During these sessions, circulate among the groups as a traveling observer and facilitator. Whenever possible, join in the discussions as an informed and interested co-participant. While you're talking with a group, make sure the rest of the class is involved in meaningful learning activities. Students who have completed their core book can also use the down time to:

◆ add information to the L (what we learned) section of the K-W-L chart;

◆ write answers to purpose-setting or study guide questions;

◆ make up their own questions;

◆ write down points they wish to have clarified or discussed;

◆ read one of the novels in the reading center;

◆ use the materials in the resource center to do independent reseach.

✳ LOOKING BACK

When all the members of a group have completed their book, invite them to particpate in a final meeting. During this session, ask individuals to share what they have learned. Then have the group write a summary which contains these ideas. A variation of this activity is to have each group member write a summary.

At the end of the meeting, provide students with a sheet that describes the follow-up activities you have chosen, or simply tell them about the activities. Allow students to choose or design their own follow-ups. Encourage them to share their finished work with the class.

You may wish to end the unit by having individuals and small groups complete the projects suggested in the PUTTING IT ALL TOGETHER section of this Resource Book. Another option is to call the entire class together for a whole group meeting. During this session, use questions like those below to tie together all the individual reading and to help students step back and reflect on what they have learned. If they have a difficult time responding, suggest that they refer to their book summaries, the L section of the K-W-L chart, and the completed Civil War time line.

- What's the most interesting thing you learned about the Civil War? What facts startled or surprised you the most?

- Of all the historical figures you read about, which one do you admire most? In your opinion, who was the bravest?

- Imagine you could travel back in time to the 1860s. Which Civil War figure would you most like to meet? What questions would you ask this person?

- What is the one scene or incident in this historical period you would like to have witnessed? Explain your answer.

- The war claimed more than 620,000 American lives. What were some of its other devastating effects? Was all the death and destruction worth it?

- The conflict occurred because the North and South could not resolve their differences over the issues of slavery and states' rights. Think about these two problems. Was war the only solution?

- What role could you have played in the war? How could you have helped to end it?

- Why do you think people today are still so interested in the Civil War?

✳ A FINAL WORD

Conclude this meeting by asking students to evaluate their cooperative learning experience.

- What did they like most about working with a group? What did they like least?

- How did this experience change their attitudes about reading and studying history?

Listen carefully to their answers. Use this feedback to help you plan your next literature-based unit. As you make your preparations, keep the following in mind: Trust the books, and trust your students. Wonderful books provide innumerable opportunities to spark imaginations, rich discussions, and students' critical reading and thinking skills. Although you may not have experienced immediate success with this approach, ultimately the rewards will surprise and delight both you and your students.

SECTION TWO:
THE LITERATURE

THE BLOODIEST WAR

by Timothy Levi Biel

*N*o war has had a more profound effect on the United States of America than the Civil War. Its outcome not only determined the political future of the country but also how American society would develop. The outcome of the Civil War has affected almost every American living today.

Between April 1861 and April 1865, the Civil War claimed 620,000 American lives, more than the combined deaths from all the other wars the United States has fought. At a time when the nation's population was only 30 million, that meant 1 out of every 50 Americans was killed in this war, or about 1 out of every 12 men and boys between the ages of fifteen and fifty.

More than half of the soldiers who were not killed were either wounded or taken prisoner. In small Northern and Southern towns after the war, crippled men were seen on every street and sidewalk. Some had lost an arm; others were missing a leg or both legs. Some towns had only a few young or middle-aged men after the war. Army regiments in those days were made up of men from the same geographic region, and in a single bloody battle, such as those at Shiloh, Antietam, or Gettysburg, all the soldiers from one town might be wiped out.

The names of these and other battles are etched deeply into the American memory. Few events have touched Americans as deeply—or have roused such mixed emotions—as the Civil War. While half of the country rejoiced at General Grant's victories in Virginia, the other half felt the sadness of General Lee's surrender. The celebration of the restoration of the Union was cut short by the assassination of President Abraham Lincoln. Every casualty was an American casualty. Every farm, village, town, and city damaged by this war was an American one, and every family torn apart by the war was an American family.

In a war filled with ironies, the greatest irony may have been the role played by four million black slaves. It was their differences over slavery that drove the two halves of the United States to war. Yet the Civil War did not start as a war to end slavery. At first, Lincoln did not even intend to end slavery if the North won the war. Rather, he wanted to force the Confederate states—Virginia, North Carolina, South Carolina, Georgia, Florida, Tennessee, Alabama, Mississippi, Arkansas, Louisiana, and Texas—to rejoin the Union. That was all. He even gave the slave owners in these states repeated assurances that he would not abolish slavery there.

It was not until New Year's Day, 1863, that Lincoln issued the Emancipation Proclamation and the war became a war to abolish slavery. Shortly after the Civil War came to a close in April 1865, the Thirteenth Amendment to the Constitution abolished slavery everywhere in the country. Although this officially ended the fight over slavery, North and South remained as emotionally divided as ever.

The first sign of this division was the assassination of Abraham Lincoln by a Southern

Library of Congress

President Lincoln visiting General B. McClellan and his staff. Photograph by Alexander Gardner, circa 1861.

secessionist just five days after the war ended. Following the assassination, the mood among most Northerners turned from triumph to vengeance. They wanted to punish the South and strip its leaders of any present or future political power. The result was Reconstruction, the period from 1865 to 1875, when Northern administrators supervised the rebuilding of state governments in the South.

A paper mill after the Civil War.

Southerners were powerless to resist this method of reconstruction. Their state governments were dissolved, their economy was in shambles, and their land was devastated by the war. Farms and plantations had no one to work them, and almost every Southern family grieved for the loss of at least one loved one. To Southerners, the North was unduly harsh, vindictive, and insensitive. These feelings remained in the hearts and minds of Southerners for generations to come. In addition, the end of slavery did not mean the end of racism and poor treatment of blacks. It would take more than the Civil War to bring about true freedom for blacks.

Today, memorials of the Civil War and of the soldiers who fought in it mark the American landscape from Maine to Texas. The gravestones of 620,000 Yankee and Rebel soldiers fill our cemeteries. The modern United States—its government, its laws, and its people—is a product of that conflict. More than 100 million black and white Americans living in every part of the country have ancestors who fought in the Civil War, who were emancipated from slavery through the Civil War, or who were forced to free their slaves as a result of that war. The Civil War shaped their lives, their society, their nation, and through them, it has shaped us.

ACROSS FIVE APRILS

by Irene Hunt

ACROSS FIVE APRILS
by Irene Hunt (Follet, 1964) Grades 5–8

▓ SUMMARY

Drawn from family records and from stories told by the author's grandfather, this deeply moving novel conveys the bitterness and drama of the Civil War through the lives of an ordinary family. The story is told through the eyes of young Jethro Creighton, who lives with his closely knit family in a farming community in southern Illinois. In April of 1861, Jethro is nine years old, and too young to understand the meaning of war. By the second April, Jethro has watched his older brothers go off to fight—two for the North, one for the South. His parents are stricken by grief and suffering as the neighbors take revenge. As the seasons change and the years pass, the family closeness dissolves, one brother is killed, and a cousin deserts the Union Army. By April of 1865, the meaning of war has become all too clear to Jethro. Although still a boy, he is forced to leave his boyhood behind.

A MATTER OF CONSCIENCE

At the beginning of the war, recruits from both sides rushed off to enlist. For others, the choices were not as simple. Like the characters in Across Five Aprils *and the following novels, they had to choose between loyalties.*

In **The Tamarack Tree** *by Patricia Clapp (Lothrop, Lee & Shepard) Grades 6–9, Rosemary is an English girl living with friends in Vicksburg, Mississippi, when the war begins. As her awareness of the brutality of slavery grows, she must choose between loyalty to her Southern friends and her own moral conviction that slavery is wrong.*

Carolyn Reeder's **Shades of Gray** *(Macmillan, 1989) Grades 5–8, is set in post–Civil War Virginia, and gives a very different perspective on the Civil War experience. After his father and brother are killed in the war, and his mother dies of grief, twelve-year-old Will Page is sent to live with his Uncle Jed. Will's anger is directed at the Yankees, and also at his uncle, who chose not to support the Southern cause. It is only when Will comes to realize how much courage it took for his uncle to follow his pacifist convictions that Will's grief begins to heal and he accepts his new family.*

Students can compare Uncle Jed's viewpoint on war with that of the elders of Zoar, Ohio, in Janet Hickman's **Zoar Blue** *(Macmillan, 1978) Grades 5–8. This book depicts the emotional effects of war upon the people of Zoar, a town settled by Separatists, a nonviolent religious group. The young men of the town are moved by Abraham Lincoln's call for troops. They defy their elders and enlist to fight, but find themselves torn by their duties as soldiers and their religious principles.*

▓ CREATING INTEREST

After you have given a brief synopsis of Irene Hunt's Newbery Honor story, point out that hundreds of novels have been written about the Civil War. Few, however, are as powerful or as moving as *Across Five Aprils*. Many things make this book extraordinary and different. The characters are completely convincing; the drama and tragedy of the war are vividly portrayed; the historical details have been painstakingly researched.

Most important, this fine work is not just a story about the Civil War; it is a book about how one closely knit family is torn apart when brother fights brother and friends fight friends.

End your booktalk by asking students to imagine what it might be like to grow up during a civil war. You might consider asking the following questions:

◆ How would you feel if the two people you loved most went off to fight on opposite sides?

◆ How might the people in your community react upon learning that one of your neighbors was fighting for the enemy?

◆ What would you think or say if one of your loved ones was accused of *treason* (betraying one's country)?

▧ MEETING ONE

After students have had a chance to share their initial impressions of this book, check to see if individual group members are having problems. Based on the outcome of this discussion, you may want to assign one or more of the following activities.

◆ A chart like the one below can be kept by students individually or as a group to record information about members of the Creighton family as they are introduced.

Name	Age	Notes
Jethro	9	anxious for war to begin; thinks war is exciting
Ellen Creighton	46	Jethro's mother
Shadrach Yale	20	Jethro's teacher, in love with Jenny

◆ Students can also use a time line to chart the numerous historical events and battles they read about. After reading, this information can be added to the ongoing class time line.

◆ Display a map of the United States in 1861. Students can use the map to mark the sites of battles as they are discussed in the novel. **Project Connection: See the U.S.A.!**, page 71.

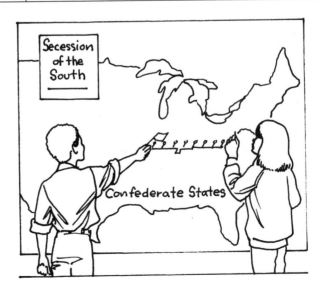

National Museum of History and Technology

Recruiting poster for the Union Army.

❄ GUIDED READING

Many of your students will find this beautifully written novel to be a fast moving and exciting read. Others, however, may have a hard time keeping track of its various subplots and the details of battles and campaigns. In addition, because this trade book is so much meatier and longer than the typical basal fare, some students will have to work extra hard to understand what's going on.

Chapter-by-chapter guided reading questions like the ones below can be used to ensure that all members of the *Across Five Aprils* group receive the support they need to comprehend and appreciate this fine work. These questions can also help you monitor and assess students' progress.

Because of its length, we suggest that this book be read and discussed in four sections. Detailed summaries of plot events for each section are given in the teaching plan below.

SECTION ONE: CHAPTERS 1–4
(April 1861–March 1862)

Historical Events in this Section

◆ Confederates fire on Fort Sumter
◆ Battles:
  Bull Run
  Ball's Bluff
  Wilson's Creek, Missouri
  Fort Henry and Fort Donelson, Tennessee

PLOT SUMMARY

Nine-year-old Jethro is the youngest child of a southern Illinois farm family. As the book begins, it is mid-April, 1861. Schoolteacher and family friend Shadrach Yale journeys into the nearest town for news. Company comes for dinner in the form of Cousin Wilse Graham from Kentucky, and dinner conversation is of the coming war. Brothers Tom and John, and Cousin Eb favor the Union; Wilse and brother Bill sympathize with the South. Later, Shad returns, bringing the news of the firing on Fort Sumter.

As spring turns to summer, news comes of battles at Bull Run and Wilson's Creek. Tom and Eb join the Union Army; John and Shad plan to leave in the winter. After months of agonizing, Bill leaves too, probably to join the Confederacy.

In February, a letter comes from Tom, who is fighting with Grant's army in Tennessee. Jethro spends a last visit with Shad at his cabin before Shad is to join the fighting.

DISCUSSING THE BOOK

CHAPTER 1

◆ How did Jethro Creighton feel about the war that seemed sure to come? Did the rest of his family share his feelings?

CHAPTER 2

◆ The Creightons were joined for dinner by Cousin Wilse Graham. Why do you think the author put him in this story?

◆ The dinner conversation turned to the pending war. How did the various Creightons feel about the war to come? For what reasons did they take the sides they did?

◆ How had the war actually begun? How did the various Creightons react to the news?

CHAPTER 3

◆ Describe Bill Creighton. What were his feelings about the war? How did he differ from his brother John?

◆ Why do you think that after hesitating so long, Bill finally left home?

CHAPTER 4

◆ How did the war go during the first year? What good news was there for the Union early in 1862?

◆ In what way did Tom's letter contain both good and sad news?

◆ What are Shadrach Yale's plans for when the school term ends? Why do you think he decided to join up?

AT THE MOVIES

If time permits, treat your entire class to a viewing of Coronet/MTI Film's 1989 video adaptation of Across Five Aprils. *This two-part presentation ("A Time to Choose and* War and Hope") *is generally faithful to Irene Hunt's novel; all of the most significant and dramatic parts have been included. As in the book, the story is told through the eyes of a young Jethro Creighton, who is convincingly portrayed by an excellent actor.*

This fine video adaptation can help those who have read the novel to develop a clearer understanding of some of the events and characters. You might also consider introducing the book through the video. Doing so can provide an opportunity for less-skilled readers to understand and appreciate the story, give older at-risk readers the confidence needed to attempt the text, and entice all students to read the book. For more information write to Coronet/MTI Film and Video, 108 Wilmot Road, Deerfield, IL 60015.

The Critic's Corner: *Whether you decide to show the film before or after reading, use this opportunity to motivate critical thinking. Begin by asking members of the* Across Five Aprils' *group to participate in a panel discussion. As the rest of the class listens, have them compare the events in the book and the film. Which events were left out of the film? Why were they omitted? Next, have students rate the actors' performances. They can then analyze the ways the film brings the book to life. Finally, ask the group which version they liked better. In all probability, this discussion will help the entire class appreciate the unique value of the written text.*

23

SECTION TWO: CHAPTERS 5–8
(April 1862–early 1863)

Historical Events in this Section

- Battles:
  - Pea Ridge, Arkansas
  - Pittsburgh Landing/Shiloh
  - 2nd Battle of Bull Run
  - Antietam
  - Fredricksburg
  - Stones River

PLOT SUMMARY

Jethro goes to town, where town "toughs" question him about Bill's joining the Confederates. On the way home one of the men attempts to waylay Jethro's wagon, but he is saved by Mr. Burdow, a man disliked by most in the area.

Pa has a heart attack and never completely recovers. Jenny and Jethro assume the labors of the farm. Jenny receives a love letter from Shad, who is training in the East. Troublemakers burn the Creighton's barn and spoil the well.

Word comes that Tom has been killed at Shiloh. In the fall, neighbors rebuild the Creighton's barn. There is news of another Union defeat at Bull Run; the public grows impatient with General McClellan.

Shad writes to tell of Antietam and Fredricksburg; John in Tennessee writes of Stones River.

This is the Union's lowest moment.

DISCUSSING THE BOOK

CHAPTER 5

- What does the conversation in the general store tell you about the community's feeling toward the war?
- How did the community look on Dave Burdow? Do you think public opinion will change after the incident with Wortman?

CHAPTER 6

- How was Jethro changed by events in March of 1862?

CHAPTER 7

- What sad news does the family receive in this chapter? Why has Jenny stopped dreaming of the future?
- Consider the list of names and events recorded in the family Bible. What does it tell you about pioneer life?

CHAPTER 8

- Who was General McClellan? What do you learn about him from Shad's letter?
- How was the war faring in the autumn of '62?

SECTION THREE: CHAPTERS 9–10
(February 1863–August 1863)

Historical Events in this Section

- Battles:
    - Chancellorsville
    - Gettysburg

PLOT SUMMARY

Eb has deserted the Union Army and appears at the Creighton farm. Jethro writes about him to President Lincoln and receives an answer.

During the summer, news comes of Union victory at Gettysburg, and of the fall of Vicksburg. Shad has been badly wounded at Gettysburg. Jenny is allowed to go to him; he recovers and they marry.

DISCUSSING THE BOOK

CHAPTER 9

- Why did the deserters present a threat to the community?
- What was Jethro's dilemma concerning Eb? Why didn't he tell anyone?

CHAPTER 10

- What two Union victories occur in the summer of 1863? What effect does one of them have on Jenny's life?
- How has Jethro's education continued, even though he has stopped attending school?

SECTION FOUR: CHAPTERS 11–12
(December 1863–April 1865)

Historical Events in the Section

- Battles:
    - Chickamauga
    - The Wilderness
    - Petersburg
    - Fall of Atlanta
    - Sherman's March to the Sea
- Lincoln gives his Gettysburg Address.
- The Thirteenth Amendment is passed, and slavery is abolished.
- Lincoln is assassinated.

PLOT SUMMARY

John writes of Chickamauga and, later, that he has seen and talked with Bill, who is now a prisoner of war. General Grant is given command in the East, and Lincoln is re-elected President.

Jethro turns thirteen as the war drags on. Finally, word comes of the war's end, and of Lincoln's assassination. Jethro mourns for Lincoln, but is comforted when Shad and Jenny return home.

DISCUSSING THE BOOK

CHAPTER 11

- ◆ What Union victories came in the fall of 1864? How did these victories help Lincoln get re-elected?
- ◆ What special news does John write to the family?

CHAPTER 12

- ◆ What worries does Ross Milton express for the nation after the war?
- ◆ What joys and sorrows does the fifth April of the war bring?
- ◆ How has Jethro changed since the beginning of the novel? What do you think the future will hold for him?
- ◆ What things do you think Jethro will remember most about these years?
- ◆ What will you remember most about this book?

INDEPENDENT READING

If students can read *Across Five Aprils* on their own, provide a study guide with post-reading questions like those below to help them analyze literary elements, such as plot development, characterization, setting, and theme. These questions can be answered orally or in writing. When students have completed the book, encourage them to add questions of their own.

1. How did Jethro Creighton feel about the war at the beginning of the book? Did the rest of his family share his feelings?

2. How did the coming of the war change Jethro's life?

3. How did the war change the Creighton family?

4. How did Jethro change from the beginning of the book to the end?

5. Which character did you like most? What adjectives would you use to describe that character?

6. What did the author do to make this character seem real?

7. Did you believe the events in this book? How did the author make them believable?

8. In this book, all of the action takes place on the Creighton farm and in the nearby town. As you were reading, were you aware that the book had such a limited setting? Why do you think the author selected these places rather than some others?

9. What is the theme of this book? Is the theme stated directly? Is it still important today?

FOLLOW-UP ACTIVITIES

Exploring Historical Fiction

Point out that there are two types of historical fiction. In one type, the characters and the story are fictional, but the setting and story events are historically accurate. *Across Five Aprils* is an excellent example of this literary type. Call on volunteers to name and describe other books they have read that fit into this historical fiction category.

Continue the discussion by explaining that sometimes a realistic fiction story is set in a historical period and actual historical figures, such as Harriet Tubman or Abraham Lincoln, are included. Can students name and describe books that fit into this second category?

Dear Diary

Ask each student to choose a character, then write that character's diary entry for a chapter in the book, or for a week after the story has ended, or for a week five years later.

From Both Sides

Use the views expressed in the dinner conversation in Chapter 2 to help students understand and summarize the various viewpoints on the war.

Ask the group to list the reasons for the conflict, as each side saw it. Encourage students to use a social studies text or the reference materials in the resource center to get more information.

A Bulletin Board

Students can create a bulletin board to represent the five Aprils covered in the novel. First divide the board into five sections as shown below. Have them illustrate each section and note events from the war and events happening to the family, such as those shown here.

ANOTHER HOUSE DIVIDED

In **Across Five Aprils** *Irene Hunt tells the story of a Northern family's involvement in the Civil War. To provide older students with a contrasting viewpoint, have them read* **In My Father's House** *by Ann Rinaldi (Scholastic, 1993) Grades 7–10. Rinaldi sets her historical novel against the backdrop of a changing South before, during, and slightly after the war. In it, she traces the McLean family's involvement in what some Southerners still call "The War of Northern Aggression."*

The story is narrated by Oscie McLean, who has grown up believing that the South need not change, and that its way of life must be preserved.

As the novel progresses, Oscie moves from childhood to womanhood. She also begins to listen to the voices of the stepfather she always resented, her Yankee tutor, a slave she's mistreated, and a brave freed-woman. By the end of the novel, Oscie sees the truth of what these people have told her, and is transformed.

The Critic's Corner: *"Many readers will find they can't put it down." That was one critic's final comment in her book review of* In My Father's House. *This reviewer also described the book as an "involving historical novel." Another critic had this to say: "Many teenage readers will lose patience with this slow-moving narrative." In this reviewer's opinion, part of the problem is that the author devotes too much time and space to the difficult relationship Oscie has with her stepfather. Share these contrasting viewpoints with students after they have completed the book. Which critic do they agree with? Can they support their opinions with specific examples from the novel?*

A Letter to Lincoln

The author does not tell us what Jethro wrote in his letter to the President; we only read Lincoln's answer. Have students write the letter that they think Jethro might have written.

❖ TEACHER'S RESOURCE

Students usually respond enthusiastically to Readers Theatre. *Social Studies Readers Theatre For Children* by Laughlin, Black and Loberg (Libraries Unlimited, 1991) can help you capitalize on that enthusiasm and bring *Across Five Aprils* to life. This useful resource includes script suggestions for Irene Hunt's Newbery Honor book and the Civil War novels *Zoar Blue* and *Rifles for Watie*. Additional suggested scripts for students to write themselves are categorized under the following themes: Colonial America, the Revolutionary War, the Settlers of the West, and 20th-Century America. *Social Studies Readers Theatre* also contains 14 reproducible scripts featuring tall tale characters and scripting suggestions for eight books by Laura Ingalls Wilder. For more information write to Libraries Unlimited, P.O. Box 3988, Englewood, CO 80155.

LINCOLN: A PHOTOBIOGRAPHY

by Russell Freedman

Library of Congress

LINCOLN: A PHOTOBIOGRAPHY

by Russell Freedman (Clarion, 1987) Grades 5–8

SUMMARY

Russell Freedman's 1988 Newbery Medal biography begins with a lively account of Lincoln's boyhood. Freedman next traces his career as a country lawyer, and his marriage and courtship to Mary Todd. The author then focuses on the presidential years (1861 to 1865), skillfully explaining the many complex issues Lincoln grappled with as he led a deeply divided nation through the Civil War. The final chapter gives a moving account of Lincoln's assassination.

Freedman carefully separates fact from the many legends about our Civil War President, and supports his well-balanced text with photos of actual Lincoln writings, as well as dozens of historical photographs, posters, prints, and political cartoons. Each of the seven chapters begins with a quote from Lincoln's own writing, and the book concludes with a collection of excerpts from Lincoln's writing, a list of historical sites associated with Lincoln, and a bibliography.

CREATING INTEREST

Recall with students that Lincoln was President of the United States during the Civil War. Point out that Lincoln is considered to be one of the greatest presidents the country has ever had, and that when he was elected he faced a real crisis in trying to keep the country together. In this award-winning biography, Russell Freedman tells how Lincoln grappled with that crisis. At the same time, he manages to portray Lincoln as a warm, appealing figure—a person we'd all like to meet. Encourage students to guess how Freedman accomplishes this feat.

MEETING ONE

As the *Lincoln* group shares its initial impressions of this biography, listen for signs that individual members are experiencing difficulty. Use the feedback you receive from this informal conversation to determine if the following activity is necessary or appropriate.

Ask students to recall some of the important things they have learned about Lincoln's life so far. As individuals continue their reading, have each one take notes on other important aspects of Lincoln's life. A web like the one shown can be used to help students record information and organize their thoughts. It can also be used to help students retell what they have learned. To extend this activity, have students

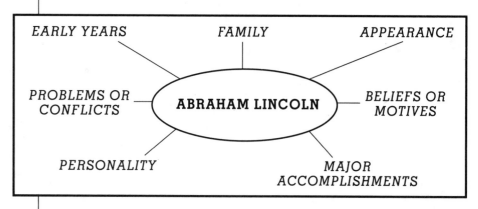

use their completed webs to write a brief biography of Lincoln. **Project Connection: Hall of Fame**, page 70.

In your initial meeting you may also want to point out that this biography is illustrated with actual photographs taken of Lincoln. Many of them were by Matthew Brady, a photographer who had a studio in Washington, D.C. Brady and the men who worked for him took photographs of battles of the war. Photography was still a new art in the 1860s. The Civil War was the first war the U.S. fought in which there were actual photographs taken of battles, and of the dead and wounded.

For more information on Brady and how he took his photographs, students can read Roy Meredith's *Mr. Lincoln's Camera Man: Matthew G. Brady* (Dover, paper, 1974) Grades 5–8.

GUIDED READING

This biography provides readers with a wealth of information about Lincoln's childhood, self-education, early business ventures, entry into politics, presidency, and assassination. To help students focus on important points and organize their thoughts, provide them with a study guide containing chapter-by-chapter questions like the ones below.

CHAPTER 1: The Mysterious Mr. Lincoln

CHAPTER 2: A Backwoods Boy

- What adjectives could you use to describe Lincoln?
- What was Lincoln's boyhood like?
- What were some of the jobs he held as a young man? What did he seem best at?

CHAPTER 3: Law and Politics

- Why did Mary Todd's relatives object to her marrying Lincoln?
- What do you think made him a good lawyer?
- Would you have liked to have had Lincoln for a father? Why or why not?

SHAPERS OF HISTORY

For a look at the life of the man Robert E. Lee considered his "right arm," students may want to read Jean Fritz's **Stonewall** *(Putnam, 1979), Grades 4–7. this is a lively biography of Thomas "Stonewall" Jackson, the South's most unlikely hero. Jackson was an orphan who got himself through West Point by sheer determination, and became the idol of the South. In telling the story of this odd man. Fritz also tells the story of the war and its impact on soldiers on both sides.*

Fact vs. Folklore: *Why do different books sometimes tell differing versions of events? Students might compare Fleischman's account of how Stonewall received his nickname (Virgil Peavey's narrative, pages 70–71) with that told in the Fritz biography. Have students do further research to discover which version comes closer to the truth.*

Three other biographies worth looking at are:

Robert E. Lee and the Rise of the South *by Cathy East Dobowski. (Silver Burdett, 1990), Grades 5 and up.*

Ulysses S. Grant and the Strategy of Victory *by Laura Ann Rickerby. (Silver Burdett, 1990), Grades 5 and up.*

Abraham Lincoln: To Preserve the Union *by Russell Shorto. History of the Civil War Series, (Silver Burdett, 1991), Grades 7–9.*

Each of these three books combines history and biography to give the readers a sense of the role a single individual can play in shaping the course of events. Each book contains useful maps and charts as well as supplemental reading lists.

CHAPTER 4: Half-Slave and Half-Free

◆ What were Lincoln's views on slavery when he was in Congress?

◆ After his term in Congress was over, Lincoln stayed out of politics for five years. What got him interested again?

◆ Who was Stephen Douglas? How did his views on the slavery question differ from Lincoln's?

◆ What happened as a result of Lincoln's election to the Presidency in 1860?

CHAPTER 5: Emancipation

◆ What advantages did the Union have at the beginning of the war? What were the Confederacy's strengths?

◆ What was the biggest problem the Union Army had in winning early in the war?

◆ At first, Lincoln did not want to free the slaves. Why not?

CHAPTER 6: This Dreadful War

◆ How did the country react to the Emancipation Proclamation?

◆ How might things have been different if General Meade had pursued Lee's army after Gettysburg?

◆ Who was Ulysses S. Grant? Why did Lincoln put him in charge of the Union Army?

◆ Why did it look like Lincoln would not get elected again in 1864?

◆ Study the pictures of Lincoln on pages 116–117. How would you describe the change in his face?

CHAPTER 7: Who is Dead in the White House?

◆ How did you feel when Lincoln was shot?

◆ What did the author do to make this chapter so moving?

◆ How did Lincoln wish the South to be treated after the war?

◆ What is the most interesting thing you learned about Lincoln or the Civil War from this book?

A NATIONAL TREASURE

Numerous photos showing events in Lincoln's life are also included in Brent Ashabranner's **A Memorial for Mr. Lincoln** *(Putnam, 1992) Grades 5–8. Interested students will also find a well-written explanation of Lincoln's legacy, a detailed account of how the memorial was built, and profiles of the architect and sculptor who created the statue that is the focal point of the building.*

Discussion Tip: In his book, Ashabranner also examines how the monument has become a powerful symbol of freedom and civil rights for millions of Americans. Students who have visited the monument can respond to this part of the text by describing their personal reactions.

▦ INDEPENDENT READING

The post-reading questions below can be used to further students' appreciation of what makes this book and its author so special. These questions can also help students increase their understanding of the man behind the Lincoln myth.

1. Like many young people, Russell Freedman grew up believing the myth that Abraham Lincoln was always good, always hard-working, and always honest. Before reading this biography, what did *you* think Lincoln was like as a person?

2. How did Freedman's book change your opinion? Is the Lincoln you read about more interesting than the myth?

3. Many biographers devote a great deal of space to describing Lincoln's courtship with Anne Rutledge. They also spend a great deal of time retelling well-known stories about how Lincoln spent his youth splitting logs in New Salem, and walking miles to obtain books. How much space does Russell Freedman devote to these stories? Do you think he made the right decision? Explain your answer.

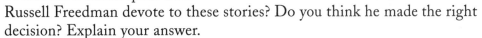

4. In his book, Freedman points out that Lincoln had weaknesses as well as strengths. He also shows that our sixteenth president was a man of many contrasts. For example:

   ◆ Lincoln was witty and talkative in company, but he rarely betrayed his inner feelings and was never fully understood by even his closest friends.

   ◆ Lincoln was a conscientious lawyer who put clients at ease with stories, but he was a hopeless slob with files and papers.

   ◆ His manner was unpolished, but he was highly intelligent.

   Work with your group to find more examples for the above list. Do these contrasts make Lincoln seem more likable and human?

5. What other evidence does Freedman use to show that Lincoln was a likable human being?

6. In your opinion, what is the best or most moving scene in the book? Describe what happened. What did the author do to make you feel you were part of the scene?

7. What is the one scene or incident from Lincoln's life you would like to have witnessed? Why did you choose this scene?

8. Imagine you could travel back in time to the 1860s. The first person you meet is Abraham Lincoln. What questions would you ask this complex man?

9. If you had the chance to meet Russell Freedman, what would you say to him?

◈ FOLLOW-UP ACTIVITIES

Exploring Biography

Remind students that a *biography* is the story of a person's life. Discuss the etymology of *biography*. (From the Greek roots, *bios*, meaning "life," and *graph*, meaning "to write.") Have students list other words containing these two roots. For example: biology, biologist, biopsy, biosphere, telegraph, autograph, photograph, phonograph, seismograph.

The title of the book they have just read includes the term *photobiography*. Why do students think Russell Freedman chose to give the book this title?

Explore how biographies are written. You may wish to cover the following questions:

◆ How does a biographer find out about the subject's life? Where does the biographer get his/her information?

◆ How does the biographer decide which information to include in the biography? Does the biographer have to "tell all"?

◆ Should the biographer tell about the subject's faults or failures, or only the "good" things?

◆ What kind of people have biographies written about them?

Library Exploration

As a follow-up to the above activity, you may wish to point out that Russell Freedman did considerable research before beginning this biography. Freedman visited the Lincoln sites in Illinois and elsewhere, as well as some of the Civil War battlefields. He also immersed himself in the literature by and about the President.

Ask students to name another significant Civil War figure they'd like to learn more about. What monuments, memorials, museums, or battlefields could they visit to find out more about this person? What books would they use to help them collect interesting information about their subject? Students can answer both questions by doing some research at the library. As they research have them write a brief description of each historical site and three or four resources they consider helpful and/or interesting. These reports

THE AUTHOR SPEAKS

Why does Russell Freedman feel it is so important to visit the places he writes about? How many drafts of a book does he do before he is satisfied? Those are just two of the questions this author addresses in **Meet the Newbery Author: Russell Freedman.** *In this live action video, viewers journey with the author to the Ford Theatre in Washington, D.C. At the Air and Space Museum, he explains how he uses photographs to "reveal something that words cannot express." This lively profile also takes viewers to Freedman's New York City home, where he discusses the writing process. Available from American School Publishers, Box 543, Blacklick, Ohio 43004.*

Activity Tie-Ins: This 20-minute video can be used to supplement one or both of the biography activities described.

can be displayed on a bulletin board or kept in an easily accessible file so that other interested researchers can refer to them. **Project Connection: See the U.S.A.!**, page 71.

Picture Perfect

"He looks so human in this picture. When I came to the end of the book, I kept hoping that somehow he wouldn't get shot and die, and I cried when it happened." That is how one fifth grader described her emotional reaction to her favorite photograph in the book, the one on page 40 that shows a pensive Lincoln with his hair in disarray. After sharing this information, call on individuals to discuss their favorite photographs. Conclude by asking students to tell how these photographs added to the biography.

You Be the Illustrator

Interested students can try their hands at writing and illustrating a picture book biography of Lincoln. The final product can then be proudly shared with some of the primary classes at your school. Suggest that students begin by examining some of the young reader biographies in your school or local library. As they read each book, they should pay special attention to sentence structure, difficulty level, and the various styles and media illustrators use to appeal to young readers.

Students can work out the content on their own. However, it might be a good idea to stress that in a picture book, the illustrations are all important. If Edith Kundhart's **Honest Abe** (Greenwillow, 1993) is available, students might want to use this book as a model. Boldly colored paintings by Malcah Zeldis vivify the story. The paintings are oversized and done in a primitive folk style. They are seemingly unpolished but genuinely American, much like Lincoln himself. **Project Connection: The War in Pictures**, page 70.

THE BOYS' WAR

by Jim Murphy

Library of Congress

THE BOYS' WAR

by Jim Murphy (Clarion, 1990) Grades 5–8

SUMMARY

Drawing widely on actual letters, diaries, journals, and memoirs, Jim Murphy paints a vivid picture of boys under the age of sixteen who served in the Union and Confederate armies as fighting soldiers as well as drummers, buglers, and telegraphers. First-hand accounts are used to describe these young enlistees' dreams of glory, the grim realities of fighting, and the horrors experienced in prisons and medical facilities. Also included is a description of the psychological affects of the war on these young men and the shock felt by families when the boys returned home. The book is illustrated with sepia-toned photographs that augment the text of this well-researched and readable work.

CREATING INTEREST

Draw students' attention to the photograph on the cover of the book. Explain that the photo shows a Union drummer boy named Johnny Clem in full uniform just after the battle of Shiloh in 1862. Then point out that Johnny was only twelve years old at the time. Explore students' reactions to hearing the boy's young age. After this discussion, point out that many boys under the age of sixteen fought in the Civil War. Some enlisted because of patriotism. Others had dreams of glory or a thirst for adventure. Why do students think Johnny joined the battle? What do they think he found?

HISTORICAL BACKGROUND

On pages 6 and 7 of his book, Jim Murphy provides a simple explanation of the political, social, and economic causes of the Civil War. In four concise paragraphs, Murphy notes the profound cultural differences between the North and the South, their opposing views on the issues of states' rights and slavery, and the South's dependence on slaves as a cheap source of labor in the profitable business of growing cotton. You may wish to use these paragraphs to review or stress the numerous complex issues that drove the two halves of the country apart and caused them to clash in a bitter war.

MEETING ONE

After the members of the *The Boys' War* group have shared their initial impressions of this book, ask them to talk about quotations and photographs that they found to be particularly moving or effective. Suggest that students use small Post-it notes to mark additional favorites. At your final book conference, these examples can be used to initiate a discussion on how and why Murphy used quotes and photos to augment the text.

GUIDED READING

The following questions on page 41 are designed for students who will benefit from teacher support while reading this information-packed book. Questions marked with an asterisk (✳) can be used to help students make connections between *The Boys' War* and *Across Five Aprils*.

The War Begins

CHAPTER 1: So I Became a Soldier

◆ Why did many young boys enlist to fight?

✳ How do the feelings described at the beginning of this chapter fit in with what Jethro and his brothers were feeling in the beginning of *Across Five Aprils*?

◆ The minimum age to enlist was supposed to be eighteen. Why was it easy for so many younger boys to be accepted?

CHAPTER 2: Marching Off to War

◆ What problems did both armies have in outfitting the new recruits?

◆ What were some of the things the new recruits had to learn?

CHAPTER 3: "What a Foolish Boy"

◆ What were the strategies of the Union and Confederate generals at the beginning of the war? How did most of the soldiers think the war would be run?

✳ Recall the first letter that Jethro's family received from Tom. How are the things Tom said in his letter similar to the comments of the boys in this chapter?

CHAPTER 4: Drumbeats and Bullets

◆ Why did the armies use drummers?

◆ What valuable services did they perform?

◆ Why would the Civil War be the last time drummer boys would be used in battle?

CHAPTER 5: A Long and Hungry War

CHAPTER 6: Home, Sweet Home

◆ Aside from times of battle, what was everyday life like for a soldier?

◆ Why do you think many soldiers became more religious while they were in the army?

CHAPTER 7: Changes

FACT VS. FICTION

To provide students with a fictional look at what life was like for boys on the battlefield, pair The Boys' War *with one of these historical novels.*

Red Cap by G. Clifton Wisler (Lodestar, 1992) Grades 4–7. Ransom J. Powell, a thirteen-year-old drummer in the Union Army, is captured and taken to a Confederate prison in Anderson, Georgia. During his imprisonment, the boy is befriended by a Confederate guard and given the job of camp drummer. Powell's courageous story is told with fairness and speaks eloquently of the horrors of war and the humanity of soldiers on both sides.

Charley Skedaddle by Patricia Beatty (Morrow, 1987) Grades 5–8. After his older brother is killed at Gettysburg, a feisty twelve-year-old vows revenge. He enlists as a drummer boy in the Union Army and eagerly awaits his first battle. Sickened by the horror of war, Charley flees to the mountains, where he meets a secretive old mountain woman and proves to her and to himself that he is not the coward he believes himself to be.

CHAPTER 8: Prison Bars and the Surgeon's Saw

- What effect do you think seeing so much killing and death had on the soldiers who survived?

- Many Civil War soldiers were buried as "unknowns." What does the Army do now to help identify the dead?

- What happened to soldiers who were taken prisoner?

- What were sanitary conditions like in the camps? What was medical treatment like?

- What do you think the author meant when he said the treatment of prisoners and the sick and wounded was "something directly out of the Dark Ages"?

CHAPTER 9: "We're Going Home"

- What were some of the feelings of the boys who returned home after the war?

- What part of this book did you find the most interesting? What startled you the most?

- What did you learn about the Civil War from this book?

INDEPENDENT READING

As *The Boys' War* group reads this book, have members work individually to list three details that support each main idea statement below. Students can then compare their lists and work together to write a chapter summary that contains these ideas. A variation of this activity is to have each group member write his or her own chapter summaries.

- **Chapter 1:** Young boys signed up to fight for many reasons.

- **Chapter 2:** Boys on both sides were unprepared for the problems they encountered during training.

- **Chapter 3:** These young men were also unprepared for the grim realities of war.

- **Chapter 4:** Drummer boys were important to both the Union and the Confederate armies.

- **Chapter 5:** A common complaint among soldiers was that there was never enough food.

- **Chapter 6:** Despite the hardships of camp life, soldiers were able to create their own comforts and entertainment.

- **Chapter 7:** As the war dragged on, the battles became longer and fiercer, and the boys were surrounded by death and carnage.

- **Chapter 8:** The treatment of prisoners and the sick and wounded was something directly out of the Dark Ages.

- **Chapter 9:** The end of the war was a time for celebration and sadness.

✳ FOLLOW-UP ACTIVITIES

Dramatic Reading

Students may enjoy doing an oral reading of some of the material in *The Boys' War*. Many quotes in the book are from the diaries and letters of the same boys, such as Elisha Stockwell, Thomas Galway, and John Delhany. Students can take the parts of these and other boys quoted in the book and do an oral presentation. **Project Connection:** The quotes could also be made part of a more elaborate presentation on the Civil War, such as that suggested in the **Civil War Dramatization** project on page 70.

Civil War Music

Several songs popular during the Civil War, such as "When Johnny Comes Marching Home" and "Tenting Tonight," are mentioned in the book. A group of students could research these and other songs of the period and perform them for the class. **Project Connection: Civil War Dramatization**, page 70.

Letters Home

Suggest to students that they use what they have learned from reading this book to write their own Civil War letters. Ask them to imagine that they are soldiers writing home to tell their families about the battles they have witnessed, or some incident in camp life.

The Statistics Are Frightening

On several occasions, Murphy uses statistics to show that the Civil War was particularly bloody. For example:

- During the first twelve months of the war, 7,000 Union and Confederate soldiers were killed. In the two months that followed, more than 10,000 were killed in addition.
- Of the 900 men in the First Maine Heavy Artillery, 635 became casualties in just seven minutes of fighting at the Battle of Petersburg.
- A North Carolina regiment saw 714 of its 800 soldiers killed at Gettysburg.

Discuss how these and other statistics helped students to understand and appreciate the horrible nature of this war. Encourage students to note down other frightening statistics they find as they read and do their research for this unit. **Project Connection: The Facts**, page 69.

You Be the Reporter

More than three hundred reporters followed the Union armies from battle to battle during the Civil War. These correspondents provided on-the-spot accounts of major conflicts. They also interviewed soldiers and prisoners of war, and sketched pictures of the people and events they saw. After sharing this information, ask students to pretend that they are reporters assigned to interview underage boys on the battlefield. Using what they learned from Murphy's work, have them answer these questions: Who would you interview? What questions would you ask them?

After students have generated questions for each interview subject, have them use what they have learned—and their imaginations—to write the answers. To extend this activity, ask students to use what they have written to compose one or more news articles. Each article can be accompanied by an appropriate sketch. **Project Connections: Press Conference** (page 71), **What's News?** (page 72).

Then What Happened?

If *The Boys' War* was popular with your students, you might want to tell them about *The Long Road to Gettysburg* (Clarion, 1992) Grades 5–8. In this book, Jim Murphy focuses on the Battle of Gettysburg, as seen through the eyes of two soldiers. Lieutenant John Dooley, age eighteen, enlisted in the Confederate Army because he wanted to defend the honor and integrity of the South. For fifteen-year-old Union Army Corporal Thomas Galway, who has experienced anti-Irish prejudice, the war is more personal. Like *The Boys' War*, this book uses first-hand accounts to bring the grim realities of war to life. It closes with Lincoln delivering his Gettysburg Address and an epilogue about the boys' postwar lives. After sharing this summary, ask individuals to tell why they would or would not want to read *The Long Road to Gettysburg*. Then challenge interested students to write an epilogue about the postwar lives of some of the boys in *The Boys' War*.

THE SOLDIER'S LIFE

Students who are inspired to delve further into the lives of ordinary soldiers and how they experienced the war may wish to read Delia Ray's **Behind the Blue and the Gray: The Soldier's Life in the Civil War** *(Lodestar, 1991) Grade 7 and up. Like Murphy, Ray uses many informative first-person accounts and vintage photos to bring to life the fears and horrors experienced by common soldiers who fought on both sides. This highly readable volume also tells about the diversity of recruits, focusing on the large number of Native American volunteers, all-black Northern regiments, and foreign-born soldiers who served in the war.*

Literature Connection: In one especially moving chapter, Ray looks inside primitive hospitals and inhumane prison camps. Have students compare Ray's treatment of these topics with Murphy's coverage.

For Further Exploration: Lessons learned in wartime dramatically improved health care when peace came. To learn how our wartime experiences helped to conquer a wide range of problems, students can read **"Military Medicine,"** *by Jane Colihan in the October/November 1984 issue of* American Heritage *magazine. This photo-essay reveals much about medical care and advances made during the Civil War, the Spanish-American War, World War I, World War II, the Korean War, and Vietnam.*

BEHIND REBEL LINES

by Seymour Reit

BEHIND REBEL LINES

by Seymour Reit (Harcourt Brace, 1988) Grades 5–6

❖ SUMMARY

This biography tells the true story of Canadian-born Emma Edmonds, who disguised herself as a man and enlisted in the Union Army as Private Franklin Thompson. She served as a male nurse in a field hospital and then volunteered as a spy. During the two years she was in the army, Emma made eleven trips behind Confederate lines, posing variously as a slave, a peddler, a washerwoman, and a young gentleman. Reit's story of this incredible spy is based on Emma's memoirs, U.S. Army records, and files from the National Archives.

❖ CREATING INTEREST

Students who have read *The Boys' War* might remember that recruitment procedures were rather lax during the Civil War. Because there were no such things as driver's licenses or social security cards, it was possible for thousands of underage boys to enlist.

Historians figure that more than four hundred women also fought in the war, disguised as men. They cropped their hair, donned men's uniforms, and fought as well as any other soldiers. One of these women was Emma Edmonds.

Explain that Emma enlisted in the Union Army as a male nurse under the name Frank Thompson. During basic training, not even her bunkmate suspected that "Frank" was a woman. How was she able to hide her true identity? After several students have had the opportunity to share their ideas, mention that Emma also served as a Union soldier and a spy. Over and over again, she risked discovery and death to secure valuable information. Based on what you have told them, ask students to supply some adjectives that describe Emma's life and story.

❖ INDEPENDENT READING

Although guided reading questions may be necessary in a small number of cases, most of your students should have no trouble getting through and understanding this simply written, fast moving biography. As a result, we suggest that all members of the *Behind Rebel Lines* group be encouraged to read this book independently. After reading, questions like those below can be used to help students think about and share what they have learned.

1. Which of the following adjectives would you use to describe Emma Edmonds? Pick three or list your own adjectives. Explain your choices.

brave	dedicated	strong-willed	driven
daring	idealistic	stubborn	hotheaded

2. List three things Mrs. Butler did to show that she was Emma's good friend and ally. Based on what you have written, what three adjectives would you use to describe this person?

3. The author tells readers that Emma was dark-haired, trim, and boyish. She had a strong chin, a firm mouth, and cool blue eyes. Very little, however, is said about Mrs. Butler's physical appearance. What do you think she looked like? Describe her in two or three sentences, or draw a picture.

4. Do you think Emma's story would make a good movie? Why or why not?

5. If you were in charge of making that movie, which actress would you ask to play the role of Emma? Who would you cast for the role of Mrs. Butler? Explain your choices.

6. Which episodes from Emma's life would you definitely include in the movie? Try to pick three. Tell why you think movie audiences would enjoy these scenes.

7. After the war, Emma got married and had three sons. Would you include this part of her life in your film? Why or why not?

8. Write an ad that could be used to persuade people to see your film version of *Behind Rebel Lines*.

▧ FOLLOW-UP ACTIVITIES

Exploring Biographies

Remind students that *Behind Rebel Lines* is a biography. Have them compare this book with *Lincoln: A Photobiography* or another biography they have read. What differences do they see between the two books? Which book do they think presented a more complete picture of the subject? Which did they enjoy reading more?

Note that in the preface of the book (To Begin, pages ix–x), author Seymour Reit explains that "certain liberties have been taken" with speeches and thoughts. In other words, he has occasionally made

> ## PASS IT ON
>
> *On the back jacket flap of* Behind Rebel Lines, *Emma Edmonds is described as "the Civil War's most incredible spy." However, many historians believe that honor belongs to another woman—the famed abolitionist Harriet Tubman. Working in South Carolina and other states, she organized slave intelligence networks behind enemy lines and led scouting raids. Students might also be surprised to learn that Tubman was the first woman to lead U.S. troops into combat.*

Emma Edmonds disguised as a slave.

up dialogue or thoughts when he could not know what was really said. Have students discuss what they think of this technique, and why they think Reit used it. Is there any evidence that Freedman used this technique in his biography of Lincoln?

Debate

Behind Rebel Lines raises the issue of women serving in combat positions in the armed forces. Have students work with their group to research various aspects of this question. Topics for research might include: women who fought in the Revolutionary War, Civil War, and other wars; the history of the WACS, WAVES, and other women's branches of the service; women in combat in armies of other countries, such as Israel; and the present-day policy of the U.S. toward women in combat positions. When students have completed their research, suggest that they hold a debate to argue both sides of this question: Should women be allowed to serve in combat positions in the armed services?

Emma Edmonds as soldier Frank Thompson.

Women and War

To learn more about the women who were vitally involved in the war, students can read *A Separate Battle: Women and the Civil War* by Ina Chang (Lodestar, 1991) Grades 5–9. This fascinating survey uses primary-source materials to personalize the stories of Louisa May Alcott, Harriett Tubman, Clara Barton, Sojourner Truth, and Emma Edmonds. Also related are the adventures of several other women who served as soldiers or spies. Chang discusses the prejudice faced by these women and ends her book with a chapter on the war's legacy of bitterness and sorrow.

Discussion Tip: In addition, Chang documents the contributions of the thousands of nameless women who made bandages and clothes, raised money, farmed the land, and taught the newly freed slaves. Use this information as a springboard for a discussion on how students might have contributed to the war effort.

QUICK TIP

To help students discover how two biographies on the same person can be different, have them compare Behind Rebel Lines *with* **Frank Thompson: Her Civil War Story** *by Bryna Stevens (Macmillan, 1992) Grades 4–6.*

THE POETRY CONNECTION

To integrate poetry into a study of Women and the Civil War, call on a student volunteer to read Nancy Winslow Parker's illustrated interpretation of **Barbara Frietchie** *by John Greenleaf Whittier (Greenwillow, 1992) Grades 1–5. Parker has revitalized Whittier's stirring narrative poem about the elderly woman who defied Stonewall Jackson by displaying the Union flag. ("Shoot if you must this old grey head/But spare your country's flag," she said.) A stage-setting preface, a map, and short biographies of Whittier and Jackson are included as well.*

Discussion Tip: Parker's preface mentions the controversy over whether or not the event memorialized in the poem ever occurred. Use this information to initiate a discussion of the fine line between history and legend.

UNDYING GLORY

by Clinton Cox

UNDYING GLORY

by Clinton Cox (Scholastic, 1991) Grade 6–9

▦ SUMMARY

As does the movie *Glory*, this book details the history of the Massachusetts 54th Regiment, which was composed of one thousand African-American soldiers and twenty-nine white officers. Cox begins his account with information on the formation of the regiment in 1863. He then follows this unit onto the battlefield and tells of its valorous struggles and victories during the remaining war years. Interwoven throughout the text is clearly documented evidence of the severe prejudice black soldiers faced, including pay unequal to that of whites and an unwillingness on the part of many in power to allow them to enter the battle.

▦ CREATING INTEREST

Point out that this book tells the true story of the Massachusetts 54th Regiment, the all-black unit that was featured in the movie *Glory*. Invite students who have seen *Glory* to talk about this film and share what they learned about the famed Massachusetts 54th. Focus the discussion on why *Glory* is a good title for the movie and on what students found out about the status of African-American soldiers during the Civil War. If you have seen the movie, participate in the discussion. If necessary, point out that when blacks first tried to enlist, they were turned down. It was not until two years into the war that blacks were accepted into the army. How does this historical fact make students feel?

▦ MEETING ONE

After members of the *Undying Glory* group have shared their initial impressions of this book, point out that much of the information in it is fascinating. However, some students may find that the author presents too many facts. If any students indicate that the density of material is a problem, you may wish to switch them to another book.

Another option is to have the entire group view the *Glory* video and scan the book, using it as a resource to add to their information about the Massachusetts 54th. Students might also watch ***The Massachusetts 54th Colored Infantry*** (PBS, 1991) Grades 7–12. This one-hour documentary is part of the *American Experiences Series*. Like Cox's book, it provides a detailed

---

PASS IT ON

Members of the Undying Glory *group will be amazed when you share the following tidbits.*

◆ *Most black soldiers—93,000—came from the South. Northern states contributed 52,000 soldiers, and 40,000 came from the border states.*

◆ *Because the War Department discouraged black applicants, there were few black officers. The highest-ranking of the 70 to 100 black officers was Lt. Col. Alexander T. Augustana, a surgeon.*

◆ *More than 200,000 black civilians contributed to the Union war effort. Most were freed slaves who worked in army camps as mechanics, cooks, barbers, teamsters, nurses, and common laborers.*

history of the heroic African-American regiment. Available from PBS Video, 1320 Braddock Place, Alexandria, VA 22314.

✹ GUIDED READING

These questions are designed for students who will benefit from teacher support while reading. Use them as "jumping-off points," and encourage students to write or ask their own questions. Be open to where the students' ideas take the discussion.

CHAPTER 1

- ◆ Why was the Union Army so slow in accepting blacks? Why were black regiments eventually formed?
- ◆ What kinds of restrictions were placed on free blacks in some northern states?

CHAPTERS 2–5

- ◆ What did blacks risk by fighting for the Union?
- ◆ How were officers usually picked for Civil War regiments? How did this differ with the 54th?
- ◆ In what ways were the 54th treated differently than white regiments? Why do you think the army was slow to use the 54th in combat?
- ◆ Why was it so important to the men of the 54th that they be used in combat?

CHAPTERS 6–8

- ◆ Why did people in some cities riot in reaction to the draft law?
- ◆ Where was Fort Wagner? Why was it important that it be captured?
- ◆ How did the Confederate forces defending Fort Wagner trick the Union into storming the fort?
- ◆ What effect did the 54th's fighting at Fort Wagner have on public opinion in the North? Which changes were still very slow in coming?

CHAPTERS 9–EPILOGUE

- ◆ What do you think was the most important contribution the 54th Massachusetts made?

A CONTINUING STORY

Older students who are interested in learning about the African-American's lot during the Second World War can consult Sylvia Whitman's **Uncle Sam Wants You!: Military Men and Women of World War II** *(Lerner, 1993) Grade 7 and up. In just eighty pages, this concise and well-researched volume creates an interesting and informative picture of service in the Armed Forces, from boot camp to the "road to victory." Whitman also notes that while some black soldiers moved into positions that were previously closed to them, discrimination continued to limit their opportunities. Blacks also had to contend with racial hostility, enforced segregation, race riots, and lynchings.*

Activity Tie-In: Students who choose to do the interview activity described (That Was Then on page 55) can scan Uncle Sam Wants You! *for background information that can help them formulate thought-provoking questions.*

▧ INDEPENDENT READING

To stimulate critical thinking, provide each member of the *Undying Glory* group with a list of opinion statements like the ones below. Ask students to think about these statements as they read. When they have completed the book, have them write down their reasons for agreeing or disagreeing with each one. Students' responses can then be discussed as a group. This activity should encourage debate and lively discussion.

1. The 54th's biggest enemy was the Confederate Army.

2. The men of the 54th fought like tigers.

3. Throughout the war, the 54th Regiment was treated as second-class soldiers.

4. The worst example of prejudice was that these men were paid a great deal less than white soldiers.

5. All Northerners praised and appreciated this regiment's valorous efforts on the battlefield.

6. After the war, their valor and fame forced most racists to change their anti-black attitudes.

7. Racism still exists in this country today.

8. If I were teaching a course on the Civil War, I would definitely make this book required reading.

Library of Congress

The gallant charge of the 54th Massachusetts Regiment at Fort Wagner, Morris Island on July 18, 1863, and death of Colonel Robert G. Shaw.

FOLLOW-UP ACTIVITIES

On the Map

Have students obtain a map of Charleston harbor and locate the Stono River and the islands and forts mentioned in the book. Note the importance of the islands and forts in protecting Charleston. Suggest they trace the movements of the 54th described in the book.

Check the Newspaper

If possible, have students read the actual newspaper stories about the 54th listed in the bibliography of *Undying Glory*. Through interlibrary loans, your library may be able to get microfilm copies of newspapers published during the Civil War, such as *Douglass's Monthly*, the *New York Tribune*, *The New York Times*, or the *Boston Evening Transcript*. Most microfilm readers can also make printed copies of specific pages from microfilm. **Project Connection: What's News?**, page 72.

FACT VS. FICTION

The story of a fictional black soldier is told in Joyce Hansen's **Which Way Freedom?** *(Walker, 1986) Grades 5–8. In this realistic and sensitive novel, a runaway slave recalls the events leading up to his present status as a private in the Thirteenth Tennessee Battalion. A historically documented account of the Battle of Fort Pillow, which took place in Tennessee in 1864, allows readers to follow the private and his regiment to the front lines.*

The Critic's Corner: *Ask students to compare this book to Cox's work and/or the movie* Glory. *Which provides the most vivid picture of the black soldier's life during the Civil War? Which did the most to help them understand and appreciate the contributions black soldiers made to the Union cause?*

That Was Then

During the Civil War, African-American soldiers had to contend with discrimination and hostility. Was this racial prejudice prevalent in later wars? Interested students can answer this question by interviewing family members and neighbors who served in World War II, Korea, Vietnam, or the Gulf War. Students can work alone or with their group to prepare a list of questions that are sure to inspire thoughtful responses, rather than a simple "yes" or "no." If tape recorders are available, these conversations can be recorded and shared with the rest of the class. As an alternative, you might invite some veterans to talk about their positive and negative military experiences. Allow sufficient time for a question-answer period.

Creative Dramatics: A Class Act

The play on pages 56–62, based on the movie *Glory*, may be reproduced. If time permits, you may want to use this adaptation to initiate a play project the entire class can participate in.

QUICK TIP

To help students cope with stage fright, talk about times when you've felt nervous or anxious. Encourage students to share their experiences.

GLORY

CAST OF CHARACTERS
Colonel Shaw
Corporal Forbes
Sergeant Mulcahy
General Harker
Thomas Searles, a recruit from Boston
John Rawlins, a recruit from Boston
Silas Trip, a recruit from Tennessee
Soldier
Supply Officer
Narrator

ABOUT THE PLAY
The Civil War took place in the years 1861–1865. It was a war that ended slavery. Thousands of soldiers from the Union Army of the North and the Confederate Army of the South died during this war. Among those fighting for freedom was America's first African-American regiment—the 54th Massachusetts Infantry. This play is based on the movie *Glory*. It tells the story of the 54th Infantry.

SCENE 1

Narrator: The year is 1861. Colonel Shaw, a young Union officer, is inspecting his new troops. They are America's first African-American unit. Some of them are in rags. Some have no shoes.

Shaw: Good morning, gentlemen. Welcome to the 54th Infantry. You are about to risk your lives to fight for freedom. People across America are watching how we do. So, let's start.

Narrator: Shaw's assistant, Corporal Forbes, tries to get the men to form groups. But they are confused. Many don't know their right from their left.

Forbes (*to Shaw*): What should I do now, Colonel?

(*continued*)

Shaw (*concerned*): Just have them start marching. I have sent for help. These men will need an experienced teacher.

SCENE 2

Narrator: The 54th marches for hours behind the white troops. Thomas and the two other African-American soldiers, John and Silas, talk as they enter the camp.

John: Did you see the white troops in uniform? I wonder when we'll get ours.

Silas (*doubtful*): They won't give a blue suit to us. Blue suits are for white soldiers.

John: But we're soldiers now.

Silas: Hey, we'll be lucky to get shoes. Where you from?

John: Boston. How about you?

Silas: I'm from Tennessee. I ran away from slavery and went north when I was 12.

Thomas (*to Silas*): I was born in Boston. When I heard that Colonel Shaw was forming this unit, I joined. He believes every man should be free. So do I.

John: My father always says, "Better to die free than to let others live as slaves."

Thomas: But some people say we shouldn't have guns.

Silas (*proudly*): I don't care what they think. This isn't just a "white man's war." It's our battle, too.

SCENE 3

Narrator: The next morning, a bugle calls the 54th to order. The drill sergeant inspects the troops.

Mulcahy (*to the troops*): How many here don't know their left from their right?

Narrator: As John and Silas raise their hands, they see some white soldiers making fun of them. Shaw watches from nearby.

Mulcahy (*pounding on John's left foot*): This is your left...

Narrator: John pulls his foot away in pain. Mulcahy shouts into his face.

Mulcahy: Now you're learning!

Narrator: As Shaw is leaving the area, he hears a voice.

Soldier: Why are you training them to kill white boys?

Narrator: Shaw turns around, but the soldier is gone.

SCENE 4

Narrator: A week later, Thomas, John, and Silas talk in their tent after having drilled all day.

John: Does Sergeant Mulcahy have to be so rough?

Silas (*rubbing his sore, tired feet*): It feels like the whole world wants to beat us down.

Thomas (*to Silas*): You're wrong. This is war, and we're not good soldiers yet. The sergeant's making sure we can stand anything.

Narrator: Suddenly, a bugle calls the 54th to order. Shaw is holding a telegram. He looks worried.

Shaw (*reading*): The Confederates have just issued an order: "Any Negro captured fighting the South will be returned to slavery or put to death. White officers captured with Negro troops will be executed."

Narrator: The troops react angrily to the news. After a long pause, Shaw continues.

Shaw: Anyone who wants to have until tomorrow morning to drop out of the Army. I will understand.

Silas (*to John*): Still want to wear that blue suit, soldier?

Narrator: John looks scared. He doesn't answer. But the next morning when Colonel Shaw comes over to inspect the 54th, all his men are there.

SCENE 5

Narrator: That next day, Shaw is eating. A supply officer sits across from him.

Supply Officer: I hear your guys are leaving the Army ten people at a time.

Shaw: Well, you've heard wrong. My men are proud to be here. Not one soldier has deserted the 54th!

Supply Officer: That figures. Three meals a day. A roof over their heads. They've never had it so good. They'll probably never fight either. Right?

(continued)

Narrator: Shaw is furious but doesn't answer. He wants to discuss something else.

Shaw (*sharply*): What about my supplies? I ordered shoes, uniforms, and guns weeks ago.

Supply Officer: Well, the few supplies we have are going to the troops in battle. They come first. (*Smiling*) You understand.

Shaw: Right, I understand more than you think.

SCENE 6

Narrator: Later that night, Forbes and Mulcahy call Colonel Shaw outside. Silas is in handcuffs.

Mulcahy (*to Shaw*): We found him deserting camp. (*To Silas*) You have committed a serious crime. Do you have anything to say?

Narrator: Silas is silent. Shaw doesn't know what to do.

Shaw: Sergeant, put the prisoner in a cell by himself.

Narrator: As Silas is led away, Thomas arrives.

Thomas (*pulling Shaw aside*): Excuse me, Colonel. You don't understand. Today, Silas heard the rumors that are going around camp.

Shaw: What rumors?

Thomas: People think the reason we don't have supplies is because we're going to be used like slaves for manual labor, not for fighting.

Narrator: Thomas reaches down and takes off his worn shoes. His feet are cut and bleeding.

Thomas: It's almost winter. We need shoes.

Shaw (*shocked*): Thomas, are all the men in this condition?

Narrator: Thomas nods yes.

Thomas: We're waiting for the day we can fight. But we can't without shoes and uniforms.

SCENE 7

Narrator: The next morning, Shaw releases Silas. Then he marches into the supply office with his biggest soldiers.

Shaw (*slamming his fist on the desk*): I want uniforms, shoes, and anything else you've been holding out on us. Now!

(continued)

Supply Officer: I already told you. We just don't have any.

Shaw: You mean not for Negro soldiers.

Supply Officer: Not for anybody.

Shaw: Well, let's see whether you haven't hidden them somewhere.

Narrator: Shaw's men start to go into the storeroom. The officer tries to stop them.

Supply Officer (*to Shaw*): You can't go in there ...

Shaw: I can. I will. And you can't stop me. Do you think you can prevent 700 Union soldiers from having shoes just because you have a problem?

Supply Officer: OK. OK. Calm down. You'll get your supplies.

SCENE 8

Narrator: The next day, Shaw watches the 54th go through drills. Their hard work is paying off. They look sharp and confident now. Forbes joins Shaw.

Forbes: Sir, the supplies have arrived.

Shaw: It's about time.

Forbes: And this came, too. (*He hands Shaw a telegram.*)

Narrator: Shaw reads it and tears it up. He looks upset.

Shaw: These men have families to support. This is unfair!

Narrator: Shaw walks toward his troops. The men, muddy and worn-out, snap to attention.

Shaw (*to the troops*): As soldiers, you were supposed to earn $13 a month. But this morning, I've been notified that Negro soldiers will be paid $10 a month. I'm sorry. Here are your checks.

Narrator: The soldiers grumble as they line up. Silas refuses to line up.

Silas (*loudly*): That's right, soldiers. Step right up! Collect your lower wage!

Narrator: Thomas stares at his check. As he tears it slowly in half, the other men begin to tear their checks, too.

Silas (*excited*): Now you're talking! Tear it up, brothers. Tear it up!

Narrator: Shaw looks at Silas and hands him a package. Silas unwraps it and finds a blue uniform.

(continued)

SCENE 9

Narrator: Finally in uniform, the 54th is sent to South Carolina, but not to fight. They are used to haul logs to the camp. Shaw meets with the Union's chief commander, General Harker, in his tent. Shaw is furious.

Harker: What can I do for you, Colonel?

Shaw: Give us a chance to fight. The 54th wasn't trained to work like horses. We were trained for battle.

Harker: That's impossible. You've just gotten here. Anyway, you didn't think anyone was going to use these men for actual combat, did you?

Shaw: Yes, we did, sir. We also know that there are some problems here at your camp.

Harker: What do you mean?

Shaw: Like missing Army supplies being sold at a local market. Who knows where the profits might be going? I hope that I won't have to write President Lincoln about this.

Harker (*nervously*): No, of course not. Actually, I was thinking your men are ready for battle.

Shaw (*eagerly*): When?

Harker: Just as soon as I can draw up your orders.

SCENE 10

Narrator: Within a week, the 54th is sent to the enemy lines. Silas stands guard with John at the edge of the camp. Suddenly, they hear a noise.

John (*whispering*): Did you hear that? We're being surrounded. You stay here. I'll tell Colonel Shaw.

Narrator: Within minutes, the men are ready. They wait for the enemy to charge.

John (*to Shaw*): Colonel! On our left, here they come ...

Narrator: The battle is short but fierce. Finally, the Confederates retreat. The 54th cheers wildly.

John (*proudly*): We did it. We drove them back!

Narrator: But the celebration is brief. Soon they see many dead and wounded. Shaw runs over to Thomas.

Shaw: Thomas, you've been hit.

(continued)

Thomas (*determined*): Don't worry about me, Colonel. I'll be fighting again in no time.

SCENE 11

Narrator: Two days later, Shaw and several officers plan a key attack on Charleston, South Carolina. The city is surrounded by enemy forts. General Harker is present.

Harker: The fort protecting Charleston is heavily armed. This is a dangerous attack. Do we have any volunteers?

Narrator: The other officers look away, but Shaw steps forward.

Shaw: General, the 54th requests the honor of leading the attack.

Harker: But your men haven't slept for days. Do they have the strength to do this?

Shaw (*proudly*): There's more to fighting than rest, sir. These men have character and strength of heart. We're ready.

Narrator: That afternoon, the 54th lines up for the attack. This time, the white troops stand behind them. They are supportive.

Soldier (*loudly*): Go get them, 54th. We're with you!

Narrator: Shaw faces his men.

Shaw: If I should fall, who will carry on for me?

Thomas: I will. We all will.

Narrator: Shaw looks at the 54th standing proudly in front of the white regiments.

Thomas (*to Shaw*): No matter what happens, we've already won.

Shaw: I'll see you at the fort, Thomas. (*He pauses, to steady himself.*) 54th Massachusetts...forward march!

EPILOGUE

Many of the men of the 54th Infantry died attacking Charleston. Their heroic attack inspired Congress to pay African-American soldiers a wage equal to that of whites. It also caused 180,000 African-Americans to sign up with the Union Army, and helped the North win the Civil War.

BULL RUN

by Paul Fleischman

Library of Congress

BULL RUN

by Paul Fleischman (HarperCollins, 1993) Grades 6–12

SUMMARY

In this unusual and innovative novel, sixteen individuals describe their experiences from Fort Sumter to the Battle of Bull Run, the first major engagement of the Civil War. The novel consists of a series of sixty brief vignettes, or snapshots, which appear as entries from sixteen journals. In these first-person narratives, Paul Fleischman gives his characters' thoughts of the moment, their actions, their fears, and their hopes and dreams.

Each character is unique, and each has his or her own reason for participating in the battle. The cast includes a gentle boy who volunteers for the cavalry because of his love for horses; a young girl whose brother enlists to escape from a physically abusive father; a coachman who has been hired to drive wealthy spectators to the battle as an occasion for a picnic; and a black soldier who enlists because he wants to strike a blow against the South and slavery. By the end of the novel, all sixteen characters are deeply affected by events on the battlefield at Bull Run, Virginia.

CREATING INTEREST

After providing the class with a brief synopsis, explain that there are two reasons why you gave *Bull Run* the last spot in your booktalk. Not only is it the most unusual of the core books in the unit; it is also the most difficult. Before choosing *Bull Run* as the book they want to read, students should decide if they're ready for a challenge. To help them make that decision, read some of your favorite vignettes aloud. After listening, call on volunteers to explain why they would or would not like to read this book.

> ***PLEASE NOTE:*** *Because of the unusual and complex nature of this novel, a special lesson plan has been provided.*

BEFORE READING

Point out that this unusual novel will have the greatest impact if it is read in one sitting. If students find it necessary to split the reading, a good place to stop is page 50. This first half of the book begins with Fort Sumter and continues until the time immediately before the battle. The second half of the book, which begins on page 51, covers the battle and its immediate aftermath.

Also point out that if anyone has trouble connecting each character with his or her previous vignettes, the small woodcuts can serve as visual reminders. Stress that students need not remember previous vignettes to understand the next ones.

MEETING ONE

After students have shared their impressions of the whole book, provide each member of the group with a copy of the chart below. Point out that there is room for information about three characters and use the note at the end of the book to locate the characters' parts. As students read each series of vignettes, they can fill in the appropriate information for that character on the chart.

Character	Side	Identity or Occupation	Reason for Enlisting	Involvement in Battle	Attitude at Beginning of Book	Attitude at End of Book
Toby Boyce	South	fifer	desperate to kill a Yankee	supposed to stay at rear, but runs off to fight	thinks war is all glory	sickened by things he has seen; runs toward Georgia
Gideon Adams	North	soldier	black man, wants to fight against South and slavery	with General Schneck's troops on sidelines	wants to fight	appalled by Union loss; itching for next battle
Carlotta King	South	slave		accompanying master to battle	hopes for Northern victory and freedom	determined to gain freedom on her own; flees to North

▣ AFTER READING

Have group members work together to combine the information on their individual charts and create one group chart. This graphic aid can be used to help students answer questions like the ones below. Remind them to use examples from the text to support their answers.

1. Which characters were enthusiastic participants in the battle? Which were reluctant witnesses?

2. What is an opportunist? Which characters would you describe as opportunists?

3. Which character had the most interesting personal history?

4. Who did you identify with the most?

5. Who did you feel the most sympathy for?

6. Pick one character. Tell how the author made this person come alive. Before you answer, think about these questions: How did the character talk? What did he or she do? What were the character's fears, hopes, and dreams?

7. A montage is a picture made by combining several different pictures or parts of pictures. How is this book like a montage?

8. The author's goal was to provide readers with a compelling look at how the Battle of Bull Run affected the lives of ordinary people. Did he succeed?

9. How does the author feel about war in general?

▣ FOLLOW-UP ACTIVITIES

That's Another Story

Review with students that a narrative can be told from a first-person or a third-person point of view. Usually, the point of view of a novel is the same throughout. Discuss with students the point of view used in *Bull Run*. (In this case, Fleischman has used first-person narrative, but instead of one character telling the story, he has used sixteen different narrators.) Why do they think the author has chosen to tell the story this way? How effective do they think this technique was? How would the story have been different if it was told through the third-person point of view?

To show students the effect that changing the narrative point of view can have, suggest that they take a section of the novel and try rewriting it from a different point of view. To do this, what must they change? How does this change affect the novel?

Understanding Dialect

To demonstrate how the author has used dialect and style to create a believable and individual voice for each character, ask students to compare pages from two contrasting characters, such as Virgil Peavey (page 17) and Dr. William Rye (page 25), or Flora Wheelworth (page 37) and Carlotta King (page 45). Introduce the term *dialect* and, if necessary, explain that dialect is the form of a common language, such as English, that is used in a certain part of the country or at a certain time. Point out that almost everyone speaks some kind of dialect. Dialect consists of the ways people pronounce words ("carr," "cah"), of different terms for the same object ("soda," "pop"), or of expressions ("Shucks!" "By Jukes!").

What differences can students find in the choice of words, grammar, and expressions used by Fleischman's characters? What do these differences in dialect suggest about the background and probable education of the characters?

Readers' Theatre

Have each group member choose one or two parts and do a dramatic reading of *Bull Run* for the class. Suggest that students practice reading the parts aloud, using a tape recorder. No costumes are necessary, but simple props, such as Confederate and Union flags, may add to the effect. Students can also use dramatic lighting, such as focusing a single spotlight on the speaker, while keeping the rest of the group in shadow. **Project Connection: Civil War Dramatization**, page 70.

The Art Connection

In *Bull Run*, Paul Fleischman has provided readers with a complete picture of each of his sixteen characters. By carefully piecing these pictures together, he has created a powerful montage of images that evoke the battle's impact on ordinary people. Interested students can create their own *Bull Run* montage. Suggest that they begin by drawing pictures of some of the characters and events in Fleischman's novel. The next step is to find illustrations and photographs that show scenes from *Bull Run*, the real

---

THE TURNING POINT

Two years after the Battle of Bull Run, Union and Confederate forces met by accident at the little Pennsylvania town of Gettysburg, in the battle that has been called the turning point of the war. The battle raged for three days and the result was horrendous—more than 50,000 men were killed, wounded, or missing in action. To provide students with a rich and varied picture of this battle, group Jim Murphy's The Long Road to Gettysburg *(see page 44) with two or more of the following novels.*

I Want My Sunday, Stranger *by Patrica Beatty (Morrow, 1977) Grades 5–8. When a young Mormon boy's horse, Stranger, is confiscated for use in the war, the boy's search for it leads him to take part in the Battle of Gettysburg.*

Thunder at Gettysburg *by Patricia Lee Gauch (Putnam, 1990) Grades 3–6. This easy reading picture book allows readers to see, hear, and feel the battle as experienced by a young girl who witnesses the events.*

The Slopes of War *by N.A. Perez (Houghton, 1984) Grades 5–8. This novel provides excellent opportunities for discussion, as the author expertly presents both Union and Confederate perspectives on the battle. The protagonist is a young West Virginia boy who faces the battle, knowing his cousins may be fighting on the opposing side.*

The Killer Angels *by Michael Shaara (David McKay, 1974) Grades 7 and up. Shaara has used historical records and the letters and personal accounts of the men who were there to present an in-depth look at the Battle of Gettysburg from the points of view of commanding officers and fighting men on both sides. Starting the day before the battle, and continuing through the three days of combat, the book is a realistic portrayal of the terror, the sadness, and the terrible loss, as well as the glory of battle. Although it is based on actual events, the book reads like a gripping adventure novel.*

soldiers who fought there, and the battle's devastating aftermath. A good place to start is the resource center. Students can scan the resource materials on display and make photocopies of the images that impress them the most.

When they feel that they have collected a sufficient number of images, they can make a rough sketch of where each piece will go, then use this sketch to help them arrange their images on posterboard. Suggest that students try several arrangements, including overlapping images, before gluing the pieces down. You might also suggest that students include a title that states their theme, or sums up the story told in their montage. **Project Connection: The War in Pictures**, page 70.

ORDINARY PEOPLE

In Bull Run, *Paul Fleischman focuses on the war's impact on ordinary people. If students express an interest in delving further into this theme, you might suggest that they read* Across Five Aprils *or Patricia Beatty's* **Turn Homeward, Hannalee** *(Morrow, 1984) Grades 6–8. In this historical novel, Hannalee Reed and her younger brother Jem are workers in a textile mill in rural Georgia, when the Union Army invades the town. The mill workers are taken prisoner by the Yankees and shipped North to work in Yankee mills. Hannalee manages to keep the promise she made to herself—that she and her brother would find their way back to their home in Georgia. In the sequel,* **Be Ever Hopeful, Hannalee** *(Morrow, 1988), the war is over and Hannalee must move again, this time to Atlanta. Beatty draws an evocative picture of post-war Atlanta, and tells a dramatic and suspenseful story in the bargain.*

SECTION THREE:

PUTTING IT ALL TOGETHER

We know we have truly understood a concept if we can restate what we have learned and apply this information in new contexts. The projects described on these pages provide students with an opportunity to do just that. The projects also afford a chance for students to make choices about their own learning, to use organizational and critical thinking skills, and to share what they have learned. Finally, they offer ways to integrate writing, art, music, and drama into the content areas. For these reasons, we consider the projects to be an integral part of this unit.

The majority can be done with information gleaned from the core books. A few will require extended research. Individual and small group projects are grouped by category and arranged by degree of difficulty. The last project—"What's News?"—can be worked on by the entire class. "Find Your Civil War Ancestor" has been provided for students who wish to do independent research.

The Facts

The L section of the K-W-L chart can be used to help students complete the following projects.

 ◆ **Is That a Fact?** Students can work alone or in pairs to prepare a quiz containing ten statements about the Civil War. Nine of the statements should be true; one must be false. Classmates can then be challenged to find the false statement and rewrite it so that it is true.

 ◆ **You Be the Author!** Ask one group to compile an "official" list of facts and statistics about the war. Group members can then work cooperatively to decide which are the most interesting, surprising, or shocking. The final list can be used to create a Fascinating Facts book. Suggest that students place one fact on a page and provide an appropriate illustration for each one.

 ◆ **What's the Question?** Another group can design a *Jeopardy*-type quiz program. To help them get started, you might suggest three categories and possible answers for each one. For example:

Statistics	Quotables	Who Am I?
620,000 soldiers	He said, "A house divided shall not stand."	I surrendered to Ulysses S. Grant at Appomattox.

After students have supplied the correct questions, they can work together to think up five original questions and answers for each category. Next, have them come up with their own categories and quiz items. Finally, suggest that group members create one or more game boards, elect a game show host, and choose three or more contestants. Their quiz program can then be "aired" for the class.

The Events

Students can use the class time line to help them complete these projects.

- **I Wish I'd Been There.** Ask individuals to write a one-sentence description of one Civil War scene or incident they would like to have witnessed. Then have them expand the description into a paragraph or more and compile their written work into a class book.

- **The War in Pictures.** Discuss how writing a picture book differs from writing a longer, nonfiction work. Then have one group compile a list of important Civil War events and arrange them in chronological order to create a picture book that can be shared with some of the primary classes at your school. Another option is to have students create a mural or montage depicting the most significant incidents or events. When the project is complete, the group responsible for creating it can present their artwork to the class and explain what each aspect depicts.

- **Civil War Dramatization.** Another group might prepare a "You Are There" dramatization in which they pretend to be reporters discussing various battles and important events. Students can also use what they have learned to stage a dramatization that includes skits, dramatic readings, speeches, and even a Civil War rap! To help them get started, work with the group to brainstorm possible ideas for scenes. Some suggestions include:
  - peoples' reactions to hearing news of the war;
  - men enlisting to fight;
  - a battle scene;
  - Lincoln giving the Gettysburg Address;
  - Lee surrendering to Grant.

Next, have students decide how to present each scene. Suggest that they vary their approach, alternating skits, musical presentations, readings, etc. They may wish to have a narrator to tie the scenes together. They may also need people to act as stage manager, prop person, and costumer. After students have rehearsed their dramatization, have them perform it live or make a videotape. Suggest that they invite parents and other classes to the presentation.

The People

- **Who Am I?** Ask individuals to write brief paragraphs about their Civil War heroes. Each description should focus on what the chosen figure accomplished. The rest of the class can use these "clues" to guess the name of the person described.

- **Hall of Fame.** Have students work in a group to make a list of famous people connected with the war. Then have each group member choose one historical figure and write a one-page biography of the person that stresses his or her contribution to the war effort. Each biography can be presented on a poster, along with a portrait-style illustration. The collected posters can be displayed in a class Hall of Fame.

To make the project a little more challenging, have students create "snapshot biographies" of their subject. Events from the person's life are shown in captioned snapshots placed clockwise in a circle. In the center, the student writes a short paragraph summarizing the subject's life.

- **Press Conference.** Most students will have seen Presidential press conferences on TV. If not, viedotape one to show to your students so they can study the procedure and the process of interviewing. Then divide a group into reporters and personalities. Personalities are each assigned the task of researching a famous Civil War figure and assuming that figure's role. Reporters prepare for the press conference by coming up with a list of questions they will ask each famous person. Celebrities must answer in character, as they think the person might really have responded. Reporters can take notes on the celebrities' responses and write a newspaper article based on the press conference. The completed article can be "published" separately or used in the Civil War newspaper project described under "What's News?"

The Places

- **On the Map.** Have one group of students create a large outline map of the United States. Group members can then work together to mark the locations of battles and significant events they and their classmates have read about.

- **See the U.S.A.!** Students can use this map to plan an imaginary trip to Civil War sites. Have them decide which state or states they will visit. Suggest that they write business letters to state tourist boards, state departments of parks, and the Naional Parks Department in Washington, D.C., requesting brochures or other information. Have them use road maps to plan their route and develop an itinerary. Incorporate math skills by having them calculate distances, mileage, and costs of gas, meals, and lodging.

- **Dear Diary.** To extend the above activity, ask students to write a travel diary of their trip.

The Issues

- **Pros and Cons.** Divide the class into groups. Provide each group with a copy of the worksheet shown on page 73. Ask each group to choose one statement to research and discuss. Before students share their viewpoints, point out that they must come up with reasons to agree and disagree with the statement. Every time they list a reason to AGREE, they must follow it with a reason to DISAGREE. They must always have an equal number of reasons in the AGREE and DISAGREE columns. When students have finished their list, have them decide as a group whether they agree or disagree with the statement. Encourage them to explain how and why they reached their decision.

- **Take a Stand.** Students can use their pro or con arguments to write an editorial that expresses their viewpoint. The finished editorials could appear in the Civil War newspaper described under "What's News?"

- **Guess Who's Coming to Dinner?** Divide the class into small groups. Then ask students to imagine that Abraham Lincoln, Stephen Douglas, a slave, and a slaveholder have all been invited to the same dinner party. The topic of conversation is the first statement on the worksheet on the following page. How might each person have responded to the statement? What might other historical figures have to say about this issue? Suggest that group members use nonfiction books in the resource center and library resources to answer these questions. When they have completed their research, have them draw up a guest list and write a play script for the dinner conversation that might have taken place. Encourage each of the other groups to choose a statment and do research to write additional scripts. When all of the groups have completed this project, the plays can be performed in class.

What's News?

Involve the entire class in writing and publishing a Civil War newspaper. A good way to start is to have students review the events on the class time line. After they have decided on the events and time span their newspaper will cover, have them think about the types of articles and features they will include. This might also be a good time to give a mini-lesson on newspapers in which you discuss the points below.

♦ Newspapers contain a variety of information in a number of different formats. Each format has a different purpose.

♦ The purpose of a **news story** is to inform the reader of the facts. All good news stories have a headline, a lead, and a body. The headline gives a quick idea of what the story is about. The lead gives the most important facts of what, where, when, why, who, and how. The body gives further details. The most important details are given first; the least important ones last.

♦ The **feature story** and the **human interest story** are usually related to a news story, but are considered to contain less important aspects of the news story. Both features and human interest stories follow the same general format: An introductory paragraph begins the story, followed by paragraphs (with topic sentences), and ending with a conclusion.

♦ The purpose of the **editorial page** is to present opinions. Editorials are usually intended to attack, defend, teach, or praise. There are a number of different types of editorials. They include editorial cartoons, letters to the editor, syndicated columns, and editorials which are unsigned. Unsigned editorials are inferred to contain the thoughts of the newspaper editors as a group.

♦ **Classified ads** may be in the form of help-wanted ads, articles for sale, housing ads, etc. Because people pay for these ads, abbreviations are used to lower the cost.

♦ Other types of articles appear in newspapers. Some of these include obituaries, interviews, reviews, advice columns, community events, recipes, and puzzles.

Name _____

| STATEMENT: | Lincoln should have freed the slaves as soon as the war began. |

| STATEMENT: | Slavery is not wrong if the people want it. |

| STATEMENT: | All of the people who fought in the Civil War were patriots. That includes both Northerners and Southerners. |

| STATEMENT: | The end result of the war justified all the death and destruction. |

AGREE	DISAGREE

Students can print their finished newspapers on a computer (several excellent newspaper programs are available) or make a bulletin-board size paper to display. Don't forget drawings and photos.

On Their Own

Here are two projects for students who like to work on their own.

Become An Expert. Many students will develop an interest in a specific aspect of the Civil War, and may enjoy doing further research on it. Encourage them to find out all they can and become the class "expert" on their favorite topic. Some suggestions:

- the first ironclad ships—the *Monitor* and the *Merrimac*
- use of balloons for aerial reconnaissance
- weapons—What guns were standard issue? What kinds of words were used? What kind of heavy artillery was used?
- uniforms—Which regiment wore baggy red pants? Which wore kilts? What insignia were used? Which officer wore a black velvet jacket? *Philip Haythornthwaite's *Uniforms of the American Civil War* (Sterling, 1985) is an excellent resource.
- battle flags—What various flags were in use?
- spies, codes and ciphers

You might suggest to students interested in the same topic to work together. You may wish to place a sign-up sheet in the learning center. Make the Research Guide blackline (page 77) available in the learning center also.

Other resources which may be helpful to students include:

- local or state museums;
- local or state historical societies;
- Civil War battlefields and battlefield museums;
- antique stores specializing in Civil War artifacts;
- local experts;
- groups specializing in Civil War re-enactments;
- magazines specializing in Civil War, such as *America's Civil War*. (The back section of these magazines have ads for everything from games to replica weapons.

Societies:
Sons of the Union Veterans of the Civil War
c/o James T. Lyons
411 Bartlett Street, Dept. ACW
Lansing, MI 48915

Sons of Confederate Veterans
Box 5164
Hattisburg, MS 39401

United Daughters of the Confederacy
Memorial Building
328 North Boulevard
Richmond, VA 23220

Children of the Confederacy
(address same as United Daughters of the Confederacy)

Sharing What They've Learned. Here are a few suggestions for ways students can share their expertise:

♦ Create an "album" about the specialty, such as an album containing drawings of types of cannon, rifles, etc., with written specifics about the weapon, such as when and where it was manufactured, how long it was used, how far it could fire, etc.

♦ Students specializing in uniforms could make cardboard figures of soldiers and dress them in uniforms representing different regiments. Or students could dress G.I. Joe dolls in Civil War uniforms and make uniforms for them for a class display.

♦ Experts on ironclads, or other ships used by the navies, could make models of them for a display.

♦ Students intersted in a specific battle, such as Gettysburg, could make a tabletop diorama of the battlefield, using papier-mâché and lichen (such as that used in model railroad layouts).

Encourage students to keep on reading and learning about their topic when the unit is over. They may develop a hobby they will enjoy all their lives.

Find Your Civil War Ancestor

Students may be interested in finding out whether they have an ancestor who actually served as a Civil War soldier. The National Archives in Washington, D.C., keeps service records of both Union and Confederate veterans on microfilm and will furnish copies to individuals upon request. If students have a Civil War soldier in their family, they may be able to get a copy of the service record.

Some students may already know of a family tradition regarding an ancestor's Civil War service, but for those who are not sure, they will have to determine when the family came to the United States. If one or more branches have been in the U.S. since about 1860 or before, they may have a Civil War ancestor!

To find out when their family arrived here, students will need to do some detective work. Suggest that they ask older relatives to help them. Next, they can consult a book such as *The Great Ancestor Hunt* by Lila Perl (Houghton Mifflin, 1989) or *Where Did You Get Those Eyes: A Guide to Discovering Your Family History* by Kay Cooper (Walker & Co., 1988).

They should then write to:
General Reference Branch (NNRG-P)
NR & Records Administrations
7th & Pennsylvania Avenue NW
Washington, D.C. 20408

Students, too, can call the nearest regional branch of the National Archives Record Center and request a copy of NATF Form 80. (A librarian can help them find the address. The form is free.)

Have students fill out as much of the form as they can. They must at least know the ancestor's name, the branch of the service (Army, Navy, Marine Corps), the state from which he served, and whether service was Union or Confederate. Military and pension records can be requested. Though both records may not exist for an ancestor, it is worth requesting both, as the information each gives is different.

They should then return the form to the National Archives. The National Archives will search the service records and send copies of what they find. Payment depends on the number of pages in the record; if nothing is found, there is no charge.

If the student is lucky, in a few weeks he or she will receive a package containing copies of the ancestor's record, which will probably include a description and information about where he served. Pension records may include information about his family, or about injuries received. If he died in action, the record may tell where he is buried. Generally, the records for officers are more complete.

Caution students not to be upset if the record shows the ancestor deserted. He may have been sick, wounded, or captured, or unable to report for other reasons. Also, many of the soldiers missing in action were listed as deserters if their bodies were not identified. Thousands of dead soldiers were never identified.

Name _____

The topic I am researching is _____
_____

Some things I hope to find out are _____
_____
_____

RESEARCH CHECKLIST

At the library

♦ Card catalog:
  Some books I can use are: _____
  _____

♦ Magazines:
  These guides will help you find out what magazines have published
  articles about Civil War topics:
      The Readers' Guide to Periodical Literature
      Children's Magazine Guide
      InfoTrac (a computerized search program in some libraries.)
  The following magazines often feature articles about the Civil War.
  (Look for them at large newstands.)
      Cobblestone (for kids)
      Smithsonian
      American History Illustrated
      America's Civil War
      Civil War Times Illustrated
      American Heritage's Civil War Chronicles

♦ Other sources:
  Filmstrips
  Videos (A good one is *The Civil War*, an 11-part series that first
  appeared on television. Your library may have it, or be able to get it
  for you.)

Further afield

♦ Bookstores: Check out the history section. Many books have been
  printed about the Civil War.
♦ Museums
♦ Civil War battlefields
♦ Antique stores that specialize in Civil War artifacts
♦ Historical or lineage societies

ADDITIONAL RESOURCES

Recruiting Posters

Reproductions of recruiting posts of famous Civil War regiments (18" x 24") can be ordered for $12.95 from J. E. Kelley & Co., Dept. A, 4 State Street, Montpelier, VT 05602.

The Civil War News

For a free sample of a 56-page monthly paper with news of preservations, reenactments, national parks, collector shows, and a calendar of Civil War events, call 1-800-222-1861.

Civil War Music

A tape cassette of songs of the Civil War, *Battlefields and Campfires*, by the *97th Regimental String Band*, is available for $10.00 from the 97th Regimental String Band, 805 Cottonwood Drive #21, Largo, FL 34643. (Other tapes as well as CDs are also available. Prices vary.)

NOTES

NOTES